VISNOSTIC™
SALES AND MARKETING

The Power of
VISualization Diag**NOSTIC**
Statements™
A Neuroscientific Approach to
Communicating, Training, Selling,
Marketing, and Leading.

Second Edition of *Visnostic™ Selling*

Kimberlee Slavik

Illustrated by David A. Wiener
Foreword by Michael T. Bosworth
Marketing Contribution by Omar Barraza
Education Contribution by Sherry Hall

DEDICATION

I dedicate all of my books to my wonderful clients for helping me understand how to make sales an honorable, respected, strategic, intelligent, and rewarding process.

SPECIAL THANKS

Thank you to the readers of *Visnostic Selling* for helping it earn Amazon's "Hot New Release in Global Marketing" on the first day it was released!

The readers that shared their Visnostic success stories are the real stars of this book! I'm especially grateful to Omar Barraza and Sherry Hall for sharing some of their success as content!

For all of the innovators and early adopters who had the insight to understand the power of Visnostics, who bravely championed Visnostic Workshops, and who radically changed their company's messaging because of it –
THANK YOU & CONGRATULATIONS!

Thank you to the Marketing and Sales Teams that leveraged Visnostics as a Team Building exercise. Congratulations for building a stronger working relationship!

To David and Donna Wiener, thanks for EVERYTHING!

And finally, thank you to my husband of over 30 years for his undying support of all my crazy, non-conventional ways of doing things. And to my wonderful son, Zachary Steele Slavik, for designing the covers of all my books!
My little family is why all this matters.

VISNOSTIC™ SALES AND MARKETING
The Power of
VISualization DiagNOSTIC Statements™
A Neuroscientific Approach to
Communicating, Training, Selling, Marketing, and Leading.

Copyright © 2019 by Kimberlee Slavik www.dynaexec.com
Illustrations by David A. Wiener

ISBN: 978-1-7331946-2-4
Library of Congress Cataloging-in-Publication is available.
Design & Layout by DynaExec
Published by DynaExec
Cover by Zachary Steele Slavik, CEO of Steele Cross Productions

Printed in the United States of America

VISualization DiagNOSTIC Statements™ Defined

Visualization

verb (used without object)

to recall or form mental images or pictures.

Diagnostic

adjective

of, relating to, or used in diagnosis.

serving to identify or characterize; being a precise indication.

Statement

noun

something stated.

a communication or declaration in speech or writing, setting forth facts, particulars, etc.

Please note that *Visnostic™ Sales and Marketing* is a complete re-write of *Visnostic™ Selling* but many important basics are repeated.

TABLE OF CONTENTS

PART ONE: LEARNING VISNOSTICS

PART TWO: READER SUCCESS/EXECUTION

FOREWORD

By
Michael T. Bosworth,
Best Selling Author
of

"**Y**ou've cracked a nut I haven't been able to crack in over 40 years!**"** were the first words I said during my initial conversation with Kimberlee. A few days earlier, she had reached out to me on LinkedIn and asked if I would read a draft of her upcoming book and if I liked it, to provide a quote for the cover. She explained that her book was complimentary to the neuroscience aspects of story in my latest book *What Great Salespeople Do*.

I agreed to read her draft, but I wasn't overly enthusiastic, because people ask me to read their new books all the time. So, I began skimming as I always do until I came to the worksheet with a list of what Kim calls Visualization Diagnostic Statements. It immediately resonated with me!

It gave me a 'buying vision' for something I have been struggling with since 1979 when I first became a Xerox sales trainer. I began (attempting) to teach salespeople how to create a 'vision of a solution' for their difficult-to-sell products and services. Contributing to my struggle over the years has been the resistance of most senior marketing executives to convert from "Product Marketing" to "Customer-Usage Marketing."

I stopped reading this book after Chapter One because as I read it, I was instinctively visualizing how I was going to use it in my Story Seekers sales training business. **Chapter One gave ME a vision of how I could finally defeat the problem of companies *leading with* product features, presentations, and demos.** I couldn't wait to begin enhancing my current curriculum with this powerful way to articulate potential product usage, so I stopped reading and got to work! And they were easy to do; I sent Kimberlee 23 Visualization Diagnostic Statements that I was able to create in less than 10 minutes. I then went back and read the book from front to back. This was the first of many times I have re-read this innovative book!

I began fighting the product-marketing problem in 1983 when I founded Solution Selling. My most passionate anti-Product Marketing campaign still involves helping sellers eliminate ONE three-word phrase that is lengthening time-to-solution expertise for their sellers as well as ruining potential customer buying cycles. That phrase is "our solution will." My Story Seekers programs teach that it is arrogant for a company to refer to their product offerings as "*our* solution" because the only person who has the authority to declare a problem solved is the owner of that problem – the CLIENT.

A huge problem, as Kimberlee points out so well in this book, is the way most B2B product marketing departments are teaching their new salespeople AND their new customers to think about their product – as an "it" – giving it a life of its own. *"IT will do this an IT will do that."* [How will IT do it? Do we plug IT in or does it have a battery?] **The vast majority of sales presentations (not conversations) are geared towards making the product or the organization the hero of the story versus the customer or client becoming a hero by solving his/her own problem *using* the seller's offering.** So, salespeople go into a presentation blasting the "virtues" of their own offerings. With today's attention spans being less than a goldfish, the result is that most buyers begin to lose their attention within the first eight seconds. With Kimberlee's approach, your first slide can have photos of the actual people in your AUDIENCE with usage statements in speech bubbles around each photo crafted in the first-person. "I have saved $2 million of my budget in just 3 months with (insert Vendor Offering)." The audience is asked to respond with one of three reactions – "I WISH I could say that today!" "I Can Say That Today" or "It's not important, I don't know, or It's not Applicable."

As an author of sales books focused on Neuroscience, I recognize why **Kimberlee's approach is brilliant – people are lazy and inherently distrust most salespeople.** When salespeople come in saying they can save money, make lives better, or make life more efficient, they are forcing the client to translate these generic statements into figuring out why they need it and how they would use it. **This book will help you do this translation for your clients!** From the first words

3

of your conversation, Visnostic Statements are written from the CLIENT's perspective, not yours! At one point, I laughingly suggested that Kimberlee change the name of this book to "The Death of Product Marketing." If this book helps to accomplish this, she will be doing us ALL a tremendous service! Every product marketing person needs to read and embrace the concepts and the science behind the way our brains respond to her innovative approach.

Kimberlee told me that a Neuroscientist wrote her original Foreword, but it was so scientific that she was concerned her readers wouldn't be able to translate the content into their level of understanding. So, let me give it a shot from my perspective. With Kimberlee's profound yet straightforward 'reframe' around how we initiate selling conversations, she is teaching us how to use neuroscience in our corporate hallways by avoiding the translation process we currently force down the throats of our clients and potential clients. The typical "We can/will save you money" seller statements (which are way too general and non-specific) force the client to figure out why they care, how they would use, and their own potential RESULTS and TIMELINES. **This book helps you migrate from your own "WE did" perspective into your customer/client hero's "I did" perspective. Our brain works completely differently when we take out the listener's need to translate from WE to ME!** "I saved $3 million in 3 months with..." is so much more impactful than being asked to believe "We can save you $3 million in 3 months with..." **When we speak in the first person, we allow the listener to VISUALIZE themselves making the same statement!** And, it puts ownership for solving the problem/achieving the goal on your potential customer/client, where it belongs. When they say, "I wish I could say this," their affirmation focuses their brain on wanting to see if it is possible. When they get proof, they want to BUY! So logical! Why haven't we been doing this all along?

Why does all this matter? Well, if you think buyers share what is really on their minds with their salesperson, you are fooling yourself. Ask any sales veteran, and they will tell you that one of the most challenging tasks a salesperson has is to establish connection and trust quickly so the client will open up truthfully about his or her situation and struggles. Hundreds of sales books have been written on this topic alone, but none have come up with a real, fail-proof way to execute...until Kimberlee's book! Visnostic Selling has wonderfully speeded up the process of getting your customers and clients to emotionally *want* your product. She has provided a neuroscience-friendly way of creating what I call 'buying visions.'

This book shows you how to replace product feature presentations with user capability statements – *Visnostic Statements*. It will enable your organization to live up to the subtitle on my 1993 book, *Solution Selling – Creating Buyers in Difficult Selling Markets*. Kim's methodology makes it as easy to buy complex technology as it is to buy a consumer product.

Visnostic Selling teaches both Sales and Marketing how to entice specifically targeted buyers with specific solution visualization statements (statements not questions). Visualization Diagnostic (Visnostic) statements allow your buyer to 'opt-in' or not. In either case, you will be happy to discover that your Visnostic statements won't trigger the typical avoidance responses most sellers elicit.

By using Visnostic Statements, sellers can facilitate potential client buying visions with a list of tantalizing capabilities where the only decision the buyer has to make is either "I wish I could say this," or "I can say this today." If these customer usage statements are targeted and tantalizing, your prospects will react to them. Once your buyers say, "I would like to say this" that statement becomes an affirmation. My wife is a therapist and has written articles on the power of affirmations. Affirmations help us manifest what we *want*. Can you think of a better motivation to buy, than for your prospects to WANT something that you provide BEFORE you even show it to them? In fact, Jennifer is now using Visnostic statements in a Relationship Quality Quiz from her own company, WeConcile. (Examples below — take the quiz at www.WeConcile.com).

Once your potential buyer makes his/her affirmations, THEN as the seller, you can demonstrate command of your company resources by getting your product experts to prove your product can deliver on that affirmation or what I call a buying vision. [Now you get to demo (finally!) but *only* the features that prove the buying vision is possible with your offering. You will have *much* shorter demos because they will be customized.]

When you combine Kimberlee's Visnostic Statements, with the power of story from *What Great Salespeople Do*, you will be able to lead buyers to the *emotional conclusions* that "this seller is authentic;" "this seller understands the difficulty of my situation," and hope that "this seller might be able to help me." Customer hero stories also help millennial sellers overcome age and gender disparities establishing trust and credibility. People make emotional decisions for logical reasons. Your product proof of vision sessions will then give your buyers the logical reasons to justify their emotional buying decisions.

The initial mission of your new Customer Usage Marketing department will be to 'harvest' the customer usage stories from your best clients and customers. The "buying visions" created by these stories will begin your library of Visnostic customer usage statements. Which can be used to intelligently position your capabilities as potential solutions for targeted buyers during sales conversations. As Neil Rackham told me in 1979, "the best sales calls are conversations, not presentations."

Visnostic Selling shows how recent neuroscience demonstrates the power of visualization and affirmation. Great leaders create a vision and lead people to it. Great salespeople help their buyers develop an empowering vision of a solution, affirm they want it *and then* help them buy it by using their technology and resources to prove it. Because these statements are mapped to simplified Statement of Works, even new salespeople will be able to explain how your company will convert non-strength areas into strengths.

After you harvest your customer hero stories, your Customer Usage Marketing Department can train new sellers on how your clients, customers and targeted buyers *use* your offerings to make money, save money, achieve goals and solve problems. Existing Product Marketing departments can transition to become the Product Proof of Capabilities department.

As you take this book to heart, I want you to try a few of these Visnostic Statements on yourself. Think about your emotional relationship with your long-term romantic partner. I am going to share some Visnostic statements from the WeConcile Relationship Quality Quiz.

For each statement, in your mind, answer one of three ways:

- **I WISH I could say this**
- **I CAN say this**
- **Don't care/NA**

"My partner and I are able to figure out how we trigger each other and resolve our conflicts."
"My partner has an understanding of and empathy for my family of origin (the family you grew up in) struggles."
"My partner understands my deep feelings and needs."

There are 7 more potential affirmations in the quiz. By making these affirmations, potential users of the WeConcile Couples Education App have a "buying vision" that increases the odds they will commit the time and energy it takes to work on their intimate relationships regularly.

Most humans like to feel in control. They love to buy and hate to feel sold to. Using Visualization Diagnostic Statements will help your clients and customers enthusiastically buy things from you that might seem "too good to be true," but that you can prove can be delivered. You control the problem, the buying vision affirmations, and the proof!

Good selling!

REVIEWS*

Of

Kimberlee Slavik's Best Selling First Book,

VISNOSTIC™ SELLING

and

TRANSLATION WORKSHOPS

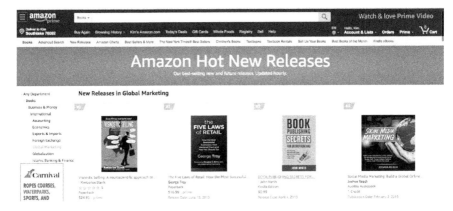

*Comments are from a diverse group of talent and experience including a Teacher, Politician, Visualization Expert, Direct Sales, Solution Architect, Channel Sales, Marketing, Ad Agency, Authors and Buyers. This book is written for everybody.

Investing time to read this section of the book will help open your mind to how Visnostics can be applied in many more areas of your life beyond sales and marketing.

Politicians, teachers, and police officers are just a few examples of readers that are leveraging Visnostics to enjoy amazing results in their respective careers.

"This is a a great read--thought-provoking, engaging and super practical. It really gets to the heart of what great salespeople do naturally, but many average performers and newer reps struggle with: the ability to create a conversation that leads TO their solution, rather than WITH their solution. I'd highly recommend Kimberlee Slavik's terrific book to anybody looking to take their selling approach to the next level."

-Matthew Dixon, coauthor of The Challenger Sale, The Challenger Customer and The Effortless Experience

Jennifer, Sales Channel Marketing & Sales Executive for a Fortune 500 Company (Top 60 with $28 Billion in annual revenue)

"With Kim's help we have been able to shift our focus from educating the customer about a specific product to identifying gaps in a customers desired end state and focus our attention on their needs versus our speeds & feeds. The Visnostic Statement method is a powerful tool to get your customers excited about the benefits without ever mentioning the products and services. It's ingenious – easy for sellers as they are simply getting to know their customer better and easy for customers because we are not asking them to make the connections between our offerings and their environment."

"As I read 'Visnostic Selling' a light bulb went off in my head; we had been doing it all wrong. No wonder the message wasn't resonating with customers, we were starting with meeting 3. By working with Kim to translate our "Meeting 3" marketing presentation into Visnostics Statements suitable for a first meeting with the customer, we are able to "diagnose" the customer and cater subsequent presentations to their specific needs (that we learn through the Visnostic Statement scoring). It's brilliant! We've turned a first meeting monologue into an engaging dialogue. Sellers love it. Customers love it. We are making it EASY and engaging for everyone. Thank you Kim! "

David Wiener, Senior Sales Leader

"During my selling career of 50 years, I read all the sales books and even taught some. I believe the perceived needs of the customer and the apparent solutions to these needs have always controlled the relationship between

seller and buyer. This, the weakest point in the sales cycle has never been fully addressed until now.

For the last ten years, Kim Slavik has worked on a method for establishing the real customer needs and their priorities. She has also created an easily understood way of establishing and presenting these needs and priorities.

Visualization Diagnostic Statements will change the way selling is performed. It is a win-win for buyer and seller. I am honored to have worked with Kim and illustrated her book."

Sherry Hall, Award-Winning Author, and Educator
"While Kim's work most certainly has the potential to be life-changing for salespeople, it also holds implications beyond the world of business. As an educator, I have seen first-hand the power of visualization. I believe Kim's groundbreaking book can create positive change across multiple settings."

Phil White former Sales VP, Computer Associates
"A refreshing common sense approach of engaging customers and prospects from their perspective. A must read for any modern day sales organization."

James "Jim" Hester, Solution Architect, Pre and Post-Sales Support
"As a pre-sales solution architect with decades of industry experience, I've noticed certain characteristics that make sales teams more successful than others. A successful sales team must listen more than they speak and absorb everything they see and hear. Although you might think I'm spelling out "Solution Selling," after reading Kim's innovative book you will find that products coupled

together do not yield a solution and customers know it. Customers want to differentiate their products and services to their customers but before they can their vendors and partners must listen, prioritize, and gain acceptance of future directions. It is too often assumed that we (as salespeople) truly understand the customer's business almost without any interaction; after all we have a solution for everything. Building and interpreting Visnostic Statements will accelerate a longer, more valued relationship with your customers putting you in the "trusted advisor" driver's seat."

Omar Barraza, Marketing Expert, Founder of PlanStartGrow™, and creator of Almost Free Marketing™

"Kim's book is the most effective manifesto for revealing the intrinsic value of genuinely understanding a person's professional and personal needs, wants, and expectations. And while her book is destined to become a 'best seller' among resourceful sales professionals, I think it is a 'must read' for anyone in marketing interested in finding new ways to communicate more precisely, accurately, and effectively with past, present and future customers and clients. That's why we now incorporate the principles of Kim's innovative creation when introducing Almost Free Marketing™ and advise our clients to leverage Visnostic Statements too."

Pamela Luke, MBA, Sales and Marketing Professional

"This powerful book is chock-full of brilliant non-conventional sales and marketing advice on so many levels. One point of value applicable to many industries is the marketing team may never be in a position to purchase the product their company manufactures. Yet, they are required to produce material that will capture the market. This requires a combination of ingenuity and great

salesmanship to clinch the deal. Kim takes the reader seamlessly through the steps needed to make the "sell" genuine in order to win while offering positive and engaging motivation."

Commander & Lieutenant
Senior Buyers for the Police Department

"Personally having no distinct sales background in marketing or technology, a company recently came in to present their offering of an internet platform they built to show how it could improve work in my field, as I represented a local municipality. I was interested in the concept and eager to see if I thought their product could improve our data collection, as were fifteen other decision makers sitting in the room. Five minutes after they started their PowerPoint presentation I thought to myself "I'm not engaged in this. I do not see why it is important to have this". Ten minutes later looking around the room multiple others had begun checking their phones or otherwise checking out. I had recently read a draft of Kim's book and had multiple conversations with her on Visnostic Statements and the benefits of engaging listeners (clients) in visualization and true feedback. As a consumer or customer I feel I have a better understanding of what to expect from a product or sales meeting and if the person who says they can provide it, really understands my needs and how their product can fulfill them.

I wish this company had read this book or spoken with Kim on truthfully and honestly engaging with the client or end user to prepare their presentation. The presenter did have a valid product they were trying to bring to the market but most likely could have improved market buy in thousands of times faster and more successfully if they had the knowledge this author or her methods bring to the table."

Bridget Cogley, Tableau Zen Master & Visualization Expert

"We can automate so much. What we can't automate is the human connection, the relationships we build and the novel - and very human - solutions we improvise. Kimberlee understands this, humanizing data and using it to find success in a manner that proves itself time and time again. So, use it to change sales, but use it elsewhere too. Where do you need to build connection and convince others?

Visnostic Selling gets to the heart of what clients want - not just what businesses want to throw at them. It lets prospects share their values, deepest dreams, and hopes, so that you - a fellow human - can bond and see a shared path in a way that no automation can provide. You know the potential solution and path your business can provide. What are often missing are the unique gaps clients see, fear, and want to correct. Kimberlee provides u system that's human-centric, allowing us to bypass jargon that's cluttered the path to understanding to get to the root of what clients need. It builds success in a way that's transformational, sustainable, and wildly successful.

Use this book to bond and to transform the process so the client shines, you support them on their path, and trust becomes the norm. Expand by letting this process become a longitudinal benchmark, allowing you to return, re-prioritize, and reach new heights with clients. Intuition and data-driven decision-making can work together."

Carolynn Boss, Senior Vice President of Sales and Business Development

"Having been in Sales more than half of my career, I wish that someone had shared this unique way of approaching a client before. I've been successful in my career but I

could have done so much more. So many times I was forced to use the Company presentation that spent 30-60 minutes bragging about the size and importance of the company I was working for and then went into deep heavy duty product descriptions that could literally put a client to sleep. Visualization Diagnostic Statements allows the client to be able to understand the benefits he would derive from your technology, understand how it will help his company (and even his career progression when he makes a great decision), while creating an almost automatic sponsor for you while doing it. Sometimes we just need to dare to be different. I find myself looking for the Visualization Diagnostic Statements that should be used for every sales conversation now."

Kelly, Account Representative, Ad Agency ($697 Million in annual revenue)

"The concept of Visnostic Statements has truly revolutionized the way I help my clients develop messaging for their brand. Kim's workshop encouraged my clients to recognize the importance of adopting a customer-centric strategy, which will help their brand resonate with prospective customers and ultimately increase sales of their products."

Harrison, Regional Sales Manager for Fortune 100 Company

"Kim's Visualization Diagnostic Statements will give my team of new sellers a scientific method for how to create content & communicate their company's value to customers. The power in Kim's methodology for my team comes from its simplicity, relatability & ease of deployment in their day-to-day.

As a management tool it helps to show where each reps' strengths & weaknesses are so I can continue to develop my people as effectively as possible. Thanks to Kim, my team & I will be more confident in communicating our value to customers."

Lynda Stokes, Politician and Former Mayor of Reno, TX

"Kimberlee Slavik has done a masterful job in explaining the art of communication/sales through neuroscience.

Reading her book is as easy as having coffee with a friend. The stories in this book and the Individual exercises help us to better understand our own thought process in order to communicate with others. As a politician I know we have just a few seconds to grab someone's attention. Kim's book will help you break through the walls we all build. In the business world I am constantly challenged to put myself out there as a product to others. This book is giving me insight and tools to build a vision and the ability to develop visions in others. Therefore, better fulfilling their needs. Putting this into play can pull somebody from the bottom of the barrel and put him or her at the top of the mountain.

PART ONE:

LEARNING

VISNOSTICS

INTRODUCTION
The Science of VISNOSTICS
WHY/HOW/WHAT

WHY you want to read this book

O nce upon a time, there was a mother and daughter. One gorgeous afternoon, these lovely women were carrying on a family tradition of cooking a prize-winning roast. The recipe was a closely guarded secret and had been in their family for decades. However, the recipe was extremely precise. The roast had to be an exact weight, the spices had to be carefully measured, the meat had to marinate for a specific amount of time, and even the weather had to be just right for the oven to work its magic.

One day as the mother was teaching all the secrets to the daughter, the roast was properly prepared and it was ready to be put into the pan. Suddenly, the mother pulled out a cutting board and cut the end of the roast off. The daughter was confused and asked the mother why she did that. The mother scratched her head and said, "I honestly don't know. This is how my mother taught me to do it. Let me call her and ask."

The mother called the matriarch and described how perfectly the roast preparation had gone and then asked for the reason they cut off the end of the roast before cooking. The elder mother burst out laughing and said, "Well Honey, I don't know why YOU did it but my pan was too small!"

I actually considered taking this story out of the second edition but it's one of the most repeated and referenced stories by the readers and it is so symbolic of Visnostics and the craziness of doing the same thing without questioning if there is a better way. The reason this story resonates with so many people is because we have all been guilty of this behavior in some form or fashion during our lives. **We tend to do things because it was the way they were always done. Every once in a while, we will actually stop and ponder why we do it and if it can be done differently. And sometimes different is BETTER!**

If I could summarize this book, this is it. You are about to learn how to do something VERY unique but there is powerful science behind why it works and why you should have been doing it this way your entire life!

In fact, you are about to embark on a journey that will change everything you thought you knew about marketing and sales. Once you have finished this book, you will be armed with powerful knowledge and insight that will inspire you to do things very differently from the way you do them today.

If this book accomplishes what is intended, you will want to review and enhance your current messaging. Visnostics will make your message much more meaningful, impactful, and memorable to your audience.

It will also change the way you purchase things because your expectations will change with how you view a sales process. As a buyer, you will ask better questions during the purchasing and exploration process.

Your message will be reconstructed to inspire your audience. You will transform your presentations with fewer words and better visuals to ensure your audience remembers your message. They will want to engage with you and share important strengths and weaknesses with you. You will be amazed as your audience becomes enthusiastic about what you have to offer them and their company.

You will NOT be asking questions. You will be making a statement that triggers visualizations. And visualization often triggers emotions. The result will be that your audience will give you more information than typically given after a question. And they will ENJOY this new approach!

People don't just buy from people they like; they buy because they become emotional about the potential solutions and the people from whom they buy.

You will experience for yourself how one simple word can trigger many different emotions and visualizations. Knowing and seeing this will help you ensure you validate your audiences' interpretations of your words. You will become aware of how our brains avoid work and how this avoidance keeps sales and clients out of sync with one another. However, you will also learn how to ensure this isn't a problem in the future.

You will learn the importance of translating your offerings into a language and delivery to which your clients can relate. You will see how this translation step strengthens your relationship with your clients because they will be grateful that you will take this translation burden off their shoulders. You will learn how to take data from your clients and translate that data into valuable information that they can use to sell you and your capabilities internally. You will learn how to create your own tools that will aid in translating pains, weaknesses, challenges, and strengths into an insightful and powerful deliverable for your client. Subsequently, you will change your life, your clients' lives, and the lives of the people around you with this new knowledge and skill!

You will change your life, your clients' lives, and the lives of the people around you with this new knowledge and skill!

———————————

WHY & HOW this book is written

Simon Sinek's book *Start With Why* is one of the most-watched Ted Talks of all time with millions of views, and dozens of spin-offs. Sinek created a drawing of three circles with "Why" being the middle starting point. He explains that most companies go right into WHAT they do but they should really start by explaining, "WHY they do what they do." A company should begin each presentation with the purpose and motivation behind what they believe.

The second outer circle should address their process and explain the specific actions they take to support the "WHY." This second step answers HOW they will do what they do.

Finally, the outer most circle and third step should explain WHAT they do. This is when the result of the WHY is explained. Simon Sinek refers to these three steps as "The Golden Circles."

However, when the artist of this book saw the circles, he envisioned that those circles were an aerial view of a Russian Nesting Doll.

For those who don't know what that is, it is a small doll that fits inside a medium doll, that fits inside a large doll. Because visualizations are a critical part of neuroscience, this graphic should help you remember the order in which this thought process flows: Why, How, and What.

RUSSIAN NESTING DOLLS

Study this graphic for a few minutes. This visualization will help you retain the order in which you should communicate with the important people in your life. You should start out with **WHY** they should care. In sales, this often is the **RESULT** of what you can do for the client. Then you will explain **HOW** you will do this. And as you will read in future chapters, the **HOW** should include **TIMELINES** because saving one million dollars **(WHY/RESULT)** in a **MONTH** is much more impactful than saving one million dollars over **FIVE YEARS**.

These first two points about **RESULTS** and **TIMELINE** are the most important words to your audience and yet they are almost always LAST or casually mentioned as a side point during critical discussions. The **RESULTS** and **TIMELINE** answer the most important question to your audience, "**WHY DO I CARE?.**" Yet just as in the roast story, this is not the normal way we communicate because we are way to programed to start with **WHAT** we do.

What is important with Visnostics™, is that it is so much more than "**VIS**ualization Diag**NOSTIC** Statements™." Once you finish half of this book, your brain should be reprogramed to THINK differently! Next time you receive or create a "marketing tool", you will start looking for the **WHY** and **HOW** instead of the **"WHAT"** we do.

VISNOSTICS™ CHANGE THE WAY YOU THINK!

I will attempt to follow Simon Sinek's thought process and this Introduction will explain **WHY** I am writing this book, **WHY** you will want to read it, **HOW** you can maximize your benefits and retention of the content, **HOW** you will execute, and **WHAT** you can do to immediately increase your income.

While this is intended to be a stand-alone reference guide, some prerequisite work will help you be much more passionate about what you are about to learn. To truly appreciate and comprehend the content, it will be incredibly helpful for you to understand the basics of Sinek's *Start With Why* because it is full of fundamental details about how the brain works chemically.

After you finish that research, look into *The Challenger Sale* by Matthew Dixon and Brent Adamson, which does an incredible job of explaining why most salespeople never get that important second meeting. It also teaches how to bring true value during your client meetings, which will guarantee that next step in the sales cycle.

Clients want you to paint a vision of how their lives and companies could be better in the future with your help.

It also does a fantastic job explaining why relationship selling (alone) is not as impactful as previously taught. It explains how to address that so it is actually the most impactful sales approach when combined with the Challenger style.

One of the things that I have found fascinating since publishing the first Visnostic book, is the backlash and debates around *The Challenger Sale*. Please ignore the skeptics and the negative comments. Yes, theorists versus salespeople wrote the book. Sadly, salespeople do not write most sales books. Why do you think that is the case? Come on Folks. Salespeople don't even like to do expense reports! Very few are going to take time to write a book! The problem with all these sales books written by non-salespeople is that they really don't know what it's like to be a salesperson. Ok. We get it. Do not allow these facts to become a mental barrier against the books I recommend because **Visnostic™ Sales and Marketing is here to help you translate all that theory into how you can actually apply it to your job, your life, and to those around you.**

While it is true that the entire concept around Visnostics™ was invented and written by a sales and marketing veteran, none of the books were written JUST for sales and marketing people! I hope you invested the time to read the "Reviews" because there are many roles that impact the success of salespeople. This book will help everybody around sales do his or her job better. So I hope you end up buying multiple copies to share because a lot of people that NEED this information, won't buy a book with *Sales and Marketing* in the title. However, these people need this help too for us to really change the way things are communicated today!

As with most salespeople, I am NOT a writer! I suspect you are going to find all kinds of problems in this book. This was such a big concern of mine that at one point I even paid an editor to "fix" my writing and after paying all that money, the book was ruined and it was SO boring to read so I trashed it! So if you want to read a book written by a salesperson, this is your book. But I am writing this book like I speak. I'm refusing to use proper punctuation, proper grammar, and I'm even going to spell things wrong. Get over it. You wanted a book written by a salesperson. Well, here it is in all its glory and imperfections. Please try and view my mistakes as a reminder that I'm not perfect because I'm one of YOU!

And finally, please read *What Great Salespeople Do* by Michael Bosworth and Ben Zoldan. It basically explains why *The Bible* is the best-selling book of all times; it is full of stories, and our brains LOVE stories! It teaches how to craft your stories to maximize the impact on your audience. Bosworth's book made so many light bulbs go off in my head that it was blinding.

It felt amazing when I realized that my success wasn't just dumb luck or good timing! I had been discounting my abilities for years. Once I understood WHY this worked, I became eager to get BETTER at what I was doing.

**I finally understood the science
behind some of the strange things
I had to do to get my clients
to understand how
I was going to help them.**

All three of these recommended books are incredible reading by themselves. However, when you combine and execute all three principles, you will harness the most powerful communication approach you have ever seen.

**You must help your audience visualize
how their life could be better in the
future with your help.**

WHY this book has more graphics and fewer words than most business books

Look closely at this graphic. Did you know that our attention spans are getting shorter at an alarming rate?

In 2000, you had twelve seconds to grab the attention of your audience. In 2015, you only had eight seconds! To put that into perspective, a goldfish has a nine-second attention span. That means that a goldfish will pay attention longer than a human today!

The same year the first Visnostic book was published, the first class of "Generation Z" entered the workforce. Studies have shown that this generation has a THREE-SECOND attention span! **That means that your first three words of your message MUST appeal to the reader instantly.**

I have worked with enough salespeople to tell you that I highly suspect the typical salesperson has an even lower attention span than a typical human!

With that in mind, the average business book has over 70,000 words and few graphics, each of my books will have less words and more graphics. **Why** am I doing that? Because I want every reader to actually finish reading the entire contents in one sitting AND the pictures will help readers remember the content!

In addition to shorter books, I will also be co-writing Visnostic "Special Editions" with experts in specific fields. These books will be about half the size because the focus will be on specific industries.

The goal is that readers will execute and receive an immediate value on a topic very important to them. Once they see the power of Visnostics, they will want to read the complete book so they can become more advanced in these very powerful new skills.

I once read about a study that was conducted on college students attending the same class, learning from the same books, the same instructor, and taking the same tests. However, one group did better than the other. The only difference was that one group attended classes Monday, Wednesday, and Friday for one hour each day. The other group attended Tuesday and Thursday for one hour and thirty minutes each day. The study concluded that the shorter the instruction, the better the retention. I'm not sure if this is true or not, but it's another data point to support my strategy of using fewer words by leveraging more visuals.

"You are Who You Are, Because of Where You Were, When" is one of my all-time favorite quotes by Dr. Morris Massey. I recommend that you familiarize yourself with this concept. Entire books have been written on this subject so we won't be able to spend much time dissecting it. However, understanding this concept will enhance your ability to have empathy for your audience. If you understand the basic concept and the importance of adapting to your audience, you will be even better at learning this new communication process. Here is a URL to help you quickly grasp the primary points of this theory – It is a video from the '80s but if you listen closely, you will realize why it's age makes the message even more impactful.

https://www.youtube.com/watch?v=_aY163kwlW4

From my perspective, I love to learn and I love to try new things. Therefore, throughout my career, I embraced the latest sales training that came out. While each book or training course was incredible because I always learned something new from each one, I also scratched my head in bewilderment. Don't writers know that most salespeople have an incredibly short attention span? Why are books so long? And why are they full of so much 'filler'? When am I supposed to have time to read all these books? Do publishers demand a certain number of pages or words to legitimize the content?

Well, here is the reality of MY world as an eager reader and student – I would get a new book, enthusiastically start reading and by about the fifth chapter, life disrupted my reading and I had to put down the book. A few days or even weeks later, when I got back to the book, I would feel the need to scan the first chapters again to get my head back in the game.

I have dozens of business books in my office and even more audiobooks on various devices. I bet I have read or listened to the first five chapters dozens of times. Sadly, I usually finished them only once! I'm embarrassed to admit this, but I am pretty sure that I have a couple of fantastic books that I never even finished! So why do that to someone else?

The goal is that with fewer words and more graphics, you will read each of my books in one sitting; this should increase the probability that you take your excitement and execute while it is fresh in your memory.

With all that said, you have purchased the "mother ship" of all my books. The content of this book includes several of the "special editions" along with reader success stories so this book is HUGE compared to the others. I hope you will forgive me for breaking my own size rule but I hope this book becomes your most treasured resource guide in your arsenal of sales and marketing tools.

In fact, I plan on having you participate in several exercises so not only will you see first-hand the power of neuroscience, you will have the confidence to do it TODAY! I also want you to believe in what you are reading. The exercises are critical so you can see these concepts work instantly. As each point is proven to you, you will become more passionate about leveraging these new skills immediately.

WHY exercises will help you learn and retain and execute more effectively

Most of you have probably seen versions of this graphic throughout your career. Which means you all should know that your ability to retain what you learn is maximized when you 'teach' the materials. Therefore, as you read, you will notice multiple exercises that are intended to simulate a teaching scenario that will enhance your comprehension.

Unfortunately, per neuroscience and human nature, you will be tempted to skip the exercises. Even though doing the exercises with other people will increase your ability to remember and comprehend the content, you will convince yourself that you are special and don't need this enhancement for adequate learning. Fight this urge!

Why waste your time reading this book if you only retain 10% of what you read? Doing each exercise will ensure you not only read, but also, hear, see, discuss, experience, and teach. By retaining 95% of what is in the book, you will not waste your valuable time reading a book that you won't remember. Over and above that, you will be more qualified to actually execute these powerful new skillsets like a PRO!

WHY Graphics are powerful

I also want to explain **why** there is a need for so many graphics. As I shared a draft of this book, I was thrilled how many people gave feedback by referring to the graphics associated with the content. Graphics help the reader retain the information!

Take a look at your current presentations and websites. Do you have more words than pictures? Do your graphics compliment your words? If not, this needs to change immediately. When graphics and words don't complement each other, it confuses the audience. This confusion will cause them to disengage.

I recently read an article on LinkedIn by Inc. called
"7 Presentation Ideas That Work for Any Topic."
https://www.inc.com/carmine-gallo/7-presentation-ideas-that-work-for-any-topic.html

First of all, I agree with every single word in this article, but I questioned the author as I read it because it instructed the reader to use more pictures than words. Yet there were no pictures. It said to avoid bullets but each point was numbered AND there were bullets. In my opinion, a bullet and a number are the same things. This made the article seem somewhat hypocritical to me and it is important that I don't do that to my readers.

My point here is that I am going to teach you how to do things and I am going to "lead by example" as much as possible. In fact, if you catch me falling short, be sure to communicate your observations with me so I can fix it in future releases! It is so easy to read HOW to do something, but it is a much bigger challenge to go out there and actually execute what you learned!

How can an author legitimize the content if the advice is not followed during the instruction?

Therefore, you will notice that almost every major topic will have at least one photo or graphic highlighting a point made in the content. This serves multiple purposes. I want you to remember the content but I also want you to find what you are looking for when you need to go back and reference, re-read, or find something.

These points are not intended to instruct you how I am writing a book; they are intended to inspire you to follow this same logic when creating communications with your clients.

Our Brains Prefer Cartoons over Photographs

You've probably noticed that all Visnostic book covers are cartoons. You've also noticed that these books are full of cartoon drawings as well. But did you know there was scientific reasons for these inclusions? There are numerous articles written on this subject so I won't dive deep into it. All you need to know is that if you have a choice between cartoons and photos for your client's presentations, you should go for the cartoons. If you want to learn more, here is a simplified article that explains the science – https://www.newyorker.com/culture/culture-desk/this-is-your-brain-on-cartoons/amp.

I have so many random facts in my head, yet I am challenged to remember who said it or from what book it came. My goal is that while you visualize the artwork, you will remember the content, and be able to quickly reference what you need in the future.

Furthermore, as I travel, teach, and present this methodology, the graphics will replace most of the words and become the focal point of my presentations to improve the retention of the content.

Visualization is a major part of the power of neuroscience.

You will also notice repetition as you read. Studies have uncovered that the mind has to absorb information multiple times and multiple ways to comprehend and retain the concept. So if you find yourself reading something familiar yet a little different, this has been done intentionally to help you retain the content.

The importance of two-way communications

As you look at these two drawings, imagine you are one of the characters in each scene. Which drawing seems to represent the most pleasant form of communication? Do you prefer to be in listen mode or do you prefer to be engaged in the communication process?

Pause as you look at these two scenes and dissect why you chose one over the other. Why is two-way communication scenario so much more attractive than a one-way communication scenario? Why do some people struggle with reading? Which scene is most like reading a book? Isn't reading similar to listening mode? Why do we need classrooms if we can just read books and learn the content?

One of the Visnostic Readers wrote me and told me about a recent graduation commencement speech. He asked his nephew what he thought of the speaker. The response was that the speech was long and boring. Isn't that what we each remember about our own graduations? Can you even recall anything that was said? Can you recall the topic? Do you realize that speeches are one-way-communication? Most speeches are long, painful, boring, and unmemorable. Do we really want this same effect on our clients? I know I don't want it to happen to my readers!

Have you ever read an interactive book? I don't think I have! I am sure they exist but they are most certainly in short supply. This is interesting because we are taught in neuroscience that one-way communications are not stimulating and they are unnatural.

This is why I will be asking you to do some exercises and to email me your stories. This may seem like a silly thing to do, but it will help you retain what you learned. It will also help you to visualize the emotions you just witnessed. It will be a good experience for you so you will be prepared to convert these approaches to your work life. The ultimate goal is that you will increase your pipeline immediately.

How much you get out of this book is up to you and is dependent upon how well you follow these instructions.

_____

WHAT are
Visualization Diagnostic Statements™?

NOTE - Also referred to as a VDS, Diagnostic Statements, or Visnostic Statements in this book.

Visnostic Statements and Visualization Diagnostic Statements are trademarked terms created by Kimberlee Slavik, CEO of DynaExec. They are statements, **written in the first person**, that require a response from an audience. They stimulate emotional responses inspiring your audience to maximize their interest in your message.   Visualization Diagnostic

Statement is the scientific term. However, Visnostics is a shorter version created by combining both words.

The statements typically <u>translate</u> features and functions into something more meaningful to the audience.

A Visnostic Statement often originates as an ineffective, generic, one-way **self-focused** message (aka **VENDOR-Speak**) that has been converted into a meaningful two-way engaging statement that is **audience-focused** (aka **CLIENT-Speak**). Existing presentations, brochures, case studies, and other marketing materials are often reworded to become Visnostic Statements.

A Visnostic Statement is also a qualification tool that will help you assess your audience. As you go through the statements, if your participant isn't responding or is struggling with responding, chances are high that you aren't in front of the right participant.

A Visnostic Statement is also an effective way to determine if sales and marketing currently have the right messaging. If creating these statements feels effortless, the current messaging is strong. When these statements are difficult to create, the content doesn't contain what the clients need and want to know.

Visnostic Statements will change the way you think. For example, I was helping a reader improve his resume and I commented that there were no results mentioned. He argued that his job didn't produce any results from his efforts. I challenged him to go research some statistics. This young man was in a support role and his relationship began with the client after a sale was completed so he didn't see how his role actually made his company any money. However, after doing some research, he enthusiastically called me back a few days later to tell me that the account he helped, paid the company over 1.5 million dollars annually. He concluded that if he didn't do a good job providing support, the company would lose that revenue stream. He now realizes his value to the company thanks to the research needed to develop Visnostic Statements.

The Importance of A Diagnostic Approach
Cause versus Symptom

So far, I have focused on the importance of the VIS in **VIS**nostics. There should be very little debate over the importance of VISualization during a sales and marketing discussion with a client. Now, let me explain the significance of the NOSTIC in Vis**NOSTIC**s.

I recently participated in a group interview for a sales leadership role. Several people described things they saw as broken in the sales organization and they asked me how I would fix these problems. The complaints ranged from sales were down to morale was low. My response to them was that they were describing a symptom and asking me how to eliminate the pain before I understood the cause of that pain. For my response, I used the analogy of a headache and how a physician would handle a patient with the same dilemma.

Prescribing a painkiller to help the headache go away will not address the cause of the pain; it will only temporarily mask the symptom. I continued by explaining that multiple things could cause a headache such as allergies, caffeine withdrawal, vision problems, medications, a hangover, hormones, a brain tumor, just to name a few. Yet each cause of these pains must be treated very differently to eliminate the SOURCE of the pain.

Just as a good doctor will dig deeper and run tests to determine the cause of the pain (aka **DIAGNOSE**), a good salesperson or sales leader should also investigate to ensure he or she is addressing the correct cause of the issues. For example, I typically interview people, review reports, analyze the competitive marketplace, and examine existing business tools in order to uncover the cause of the problem.

Too often enthusiastic and new sales professionals will start attempting to fix the symptom versus taking the necessary extra time to uncover the cause of the issues. This happens with internal pains as well as client pains.

Not until a successful **diagnosis** of the **cause** of the pain is made, can the appropriate plan of action be executed to eliminate the **source** of the pain.

Visnostic Statements should be constructed to identify your clients' pains and the cause of their pains. It is the responsibility of the sales organization to differentiate pains, challenges, and weaknesses as either causes or symptoms.

Converting typical sales points into this unique format will engage your client and create the desire to share important details that will help properly diagnose the cause and how the client can be helped.

The most important step for a salesperson during a sales cycle is diagnosing the client's needs. VisNOSTICS makes this step much more accurate, efficient, and effective than just asking questions.

Why This Is Relevant and Important

If a salesperson is taught a presentation and delivers the presentation on sales calls, do they really understand the client's source of the pain?

Converting marketing content into "Visnostic Statements" is the first step in creating a powerful tool that will help diagnose the most effective areas in which the sales team can help the client. Visnostic Statements will create an environment that will stimulate meaningful and valuable conversations with the client.

WHAT Buyers Learn

I knew this book would benefit sales professionals, marketing teams, sales leaders, and any other client-facing roles in an organization. I never envisioned that BUYERS would find the content of value. However, as I was having close friends and family review the draft, I received some unexpected feedback from two people with zero sales backgrounds. While they didn't sell for a living, they did have frequent purchasing requirements and were often forced to endure some pretty tough and painful sales presentations.

I was excited to hear that a few weeks after reading a draft, a very important sales presentation was conducted. People that had a vested interest in learning more about the offering attended the meeting. These two people just happened to be in the same presentation and they told me they viewed the salespeople very differently after learning about the concepts around Visnostic Statements.

They explained that they were on opposite sides of the room, texting each other about how horrible the slides were. They were full of words and bullets and had very few graphics that made sense. They looked around the room and observed the entire audience was disengaged and on their various smart devices. The salespeople had lost the interest of the entire room and now my two friends understood why the presentation was not effective!

These two people went on to explain that they are stronger and more educated buyers after reading the draft. They continued explaining that their expectations are higher than they were before reading the book. They also suggested that I reach out to the company that presented to them because they actually want to buy the offering. However, the salespeople simply didn't build a strong enough case to justify the purchase! This is such terrific insight from Buyers! Therefore, try and imagine how your clients would react to the content you are reading. What would YOUR clients say about YOUR interaction with them?

VDS are Universally Effective

Even though my career has been primarily associated with Silicon Valley companies, Visnostic Statements should apply to all sales and marketing scenarios. For example, if you are a Real Estate Agent and you sell houses based upon the number of bedrooms, bathrooms, square footage, and price, you will sell more if you lead with the real reason clients actually buy homes, which is HOW HAPPY THEY WILL BE AS THEY LIVE IN IT. One of the greatest Agents I ever worked with told me that she didn't sell homes; she sold dreams. Creating effective VDS will flush out those dreams and help potential home buyers VISUALIZE themselves living in your new listing.

I'm also working with a paint company that insists their buyers buy on price and relationships. They believe that all of their buyers consider paint to be a commodity. My response to this comment was, **"If your clients view your offerings as a commodity, you are SELLING it as a commodity; VDS will highlight the differentiators that will help change this perspective for both salespeople AND clients."**

One final story I want to share with you is around the "WHY" of this book. When I was in High School, I had a friend that had beautiful blond hair and I am a brunette. I couldn't help notice that the boys were much more intrigued by her than me and I was convinced it was due to her gorgeous blond hair. She told me that she used something called "Sun In" on her hair. So I went to the store to get some but I noticed the bottle said, "Do not use on dark hair." But it didn't say WHY so I bought it anyway. I sprayed my hair and went out in the sun as instructed. Well, those that grew up when I did already know how this turned out for me. My hair turned ORANGE! I was mortified. So to avoid embarrassment, I put on a hat and went back to the store to buy something that would put my hair back to its original color. However, every box said, "Do not use on bleached hair." But none of the boxes explained WHY. So I bought it anyway...Y'all should already know that this story didn't turn out well for me...my hair turned PURPLE! And this was back when purple hair was NOT COOL!

The moral to this story is that understanding WHY we do things is an important part of life. I have attempted to explain as many "WHYs" as I could in this introduction; you now know WHY this book was written, WHY you should follow the instructions, and WHY it is formatted in an unusual way. You also now understand HOW to get the most out of what you read, and WHAT the outcome should be for you, your company, and your clients.

But I am painfully aware that I am far from perfect so as you read this book, if you find yourself wondering WHY about anything, please reach out to me immediately. Because, despite how cool colorful hair is today, I don't want any readers to end up with orange or purple hair unless it's intentional.

CHAPTER ONE
THE HISTORY OF VISNOSTICS

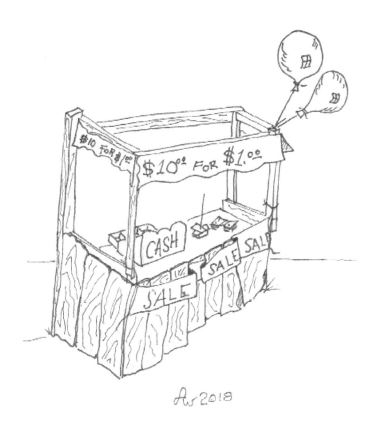

In 2004 I represented a company and a service that I was so passionate about that I invested in the company. I sincerely believed that I had ten-dollar bills for sale for just one dollar.

Think about that! If someone gave you a stack of ten-dollar bills and told you that they would pay you commissions to go sell them for one dollar, wouldn't you call every person you knew? Wouldn't you jump out of bed in the morning and go on sales calls with tremendous enthusiasm? I was setting up at least five meetings each day and I would have done more but I ran out of daylight. I still hold sales records at that company! That was my life for the first decade of my career and I sincerely believed that my customers loved me for educating them on what I was selling.

However, there was this one client that shocked and frustrated me because he didn't seem to see the value I brought to him and his company. This is the story of how Visualization Diagnostic Statements were born.

The first time I presented to him, he fell asleep. HE FELL ASLEEP! Of course, he was embarrassed and set up another meeting. I was actually encouraged during the second meeting because I noticed him taking very vigorous notes. He seemed to be really concentrating and really into what he was writing down. I walked over to him and he was doing his grocery list. HE WAS DOING HIS GROCERY LIST!

shopping list

produce	dairy	dry
apples	yogurt	peanut butter
bananas	butter	canned tomato
lemons	eggs	pasta
spinach	kefier	black beans
kale		
celery		
cucumber	meat	misc
yams	chicken	t.p.
red onion		la croix
garlic		laundry det.

I was young and so bewildered that someone wasn't paying attention to me! After all, I WAS SELLING TEN DOLLAR BILLS FOR JUST ONE DOLLAR! I had lost him for the second time and I was frustrated because I had been working with him for a year. What added to this frustration was that I KNEW he would love me for what I could do for him! How could he not want to pay attention to what I had to say?

I actually stopped the presentation and pleaded with him to tell me what I was doing wrong. He said nothing was wrong.

He then stated that he had to be honest with me; he didn't have a budget to buy anything so he was just meeting with me to be nice. (Why do clients think that wasting our time and disrespecting us as Professionals is being nice?)

At that moment, I knew I had to approach things very differently for him to digest how I could rock his world with my service. He told me that he was sorry that he wasted my time. I thanked him for his honesty and I left but I didn't stop thinking about what he said and what I did NOT say.

One of my personal mottos is "No" means "Try Harder." So I accepted the fact that I was accountable for this failure because I was doing something ineffective and I needed to try harder, or in this case I needed to try something different.

I was convinced that my presentation just wasn't keeping his attention. I thought of all the things that I should have said to him while I was there. My software didn't need a budget because the return on investment was extremely high and it was fast.

How could I go back to him and deliver this message differently? How could I get him to listen to me? A third presentation was out of the question. Why wasn't this working? It was the same deck I used to sell everybody else so why didn't this guy get excited too?

I don't know how I came up with this idea. I don't think I am that smart so it must have been some type of divine intervention. I took a close look at my presentation and for the first time, I really dissected what each bullet said. Wow. This was terrible! How have I been so blind for so long?

I tried to put myself in my client's shoes and read my presentation through his eyes. I never really looked at my messaging through my clients' eyes. I always viewed my presentation as MY story and MY COMPANY's story.

I noticed for the first time that each bullet sounded so generic. I sounded like each of my competitors. In fact, the wording was so general in nature that I could have been selling anything. What did my client really want to know? He wants to know how I will make his life better! But my presentation was very detailed on how I did things and what I did. Then it dawned on me – SOMETHING MAJOR WAS MISSING!

I then reviewed our other marketing tools such as brochures, web pages, advertisements, infographics, and anything else I could find that explained the details around our other client successes. For the first time, I found myself looking for RESULTS and I realized that they were extremely difficult to find in our current "sales tools!" I suddenly realized that my client had his own story and his own problems. Which is why he didn't care about my company story!

I needed to change MY story into HIS story!

I reworded each marketing point. Instead of approaching the communication with "this is what WE can do for you," I changed the wording to be a statement that HE would make. "My company can back up your data in a fraction of the time you are spending today" changed to "I will save a million dollars by backing up my data in a fraction of the time!"

I was going to ask him if he wished he could say these things today. After he confirmed he wished he could say them, I suspected that THEN he would want to know more about my company and how we do things! I had been doing things out of order! I had been telling clients what we did and so far, my clients were able to translate *what I did*, into *why they cared*. This guy needed me to do that translation for him!

When I first created these statements, I called them "Challenge Statements." However, when I started to document my experiences, I researched that term. I discovered that the definitions and descriptions were an established legal term. And the existing definition did not align with what I was doing. I worried that referring to these phrases, as Challenge Statements, would cause too much confusion.

So I changed the term to "Diagnostic Statements" but quickly discovered this was also an established term used in nursing.

It is because of these past name changes that, "Visualization Diagnostic Statements" has been trademarked. While this current term better describes the science behind what is accomplished, unfortunately, it was a mouthful and difficult to say. **Therefore, by combining Visualization and Diagnostics, the word, Visnostics was born and trademarked!**

I am explaining this because in a few pages, you will see a copy of the original document. I want to avoid any confusion the different terms may cause the readers. Challenge Statements, Visnostic Statements, Diagnostic Statements, Visualization Diagnostic Statements, and VDS are the same thing. Both the name and the process have evolved throughout the years.

I then made four columns in a Word document. I labeled these columns "Would like to say this," "Say this today," "NA, Not important, or do not know" and "Challenge Statement."

Next, I took each presentation bullet describing the features/functions/benefits of what I was selling and made each bullet a line item. But first I translated them from "We can do this..." into "I can do this..." These became the first "Challenge Statements."

Once this new document was completed, I called the client back and asked him to go to lunch with me. At first, he resisted and reminded me that he didn't have a budget and wasn't going to buy from me. I reassured him that I heard that message loud and clear in our meeting, but I really needed a favor. I promised not to try selling him anything. I just needed his advice on how I could do things better in the future.

I explained that I had created something new that I wanted to share and then listen to his valuable feedback. Once he knew I wasn't trying to sell him, he agreed to lunch. I suspect there may even be a chapter in neuroscience about our eagerness to respond when someone needs our help.

I could actually feel his defensive walls come crashing down. I'm not sure if it was the offer of a free lunch, the promise that I wasn't going to try and sell him again, or that I needed his help that got me that third meeting. But I do know that his "Fight or Flight" instinct had been disengaged and this was a huge step in correcting what had gone wrong during the first two meetings.

Once we were at lunch and had our food, I pushed my plate aside. I apologized to him for trying to force a presentation. I explained that this time I had a different approach that didn't require a projector, conference room, or even a laptop.

Two Way Communication

All I had was a piece of paper with printing on one side. I told him that I was going to make a statement and with each statement, I would need him to respond with one of three responses. "I can do this today," "I wish I could do this today," or "I don't know, not important, not applicable."

NOTE: After reading this book, Bosworth began referring to these client responses as "AFFIRMATIONS" and he actually wrote about these affirmations in the Foreword. However, be careful not to confuse the client affirmations with the actual statements. A statement is always a statement even after the client responds, but not all client responses will be affirmations. For example, if a client responds to the statement, "not important" or "not applicable," the client response is NOT an affirmation. However, the statement is still a statement. This is an important principle to understand while reading this book.

He agreed and I started with the first line. "Restore is a simple and visual process." His eyes immediately looked up and to the left; I was stunned. I had been taught that salespeople should look for this body language because it meant that the audience was envisioning something that would get them emotionally engaged in the conversation.

To my surprise, not only did he say he WISHED he could do that today, he elaborated on how they did it today and how long it took and how painful it was. He even told me a recent story about how the CEO had accidentally deleted an email. The CEO frantically called the IT department and explained that this was an emergency and he needed them to restore that email immediately.

However, it took over twenty-four hours to find the backup of the deleted email and restore it. This was such a serious issue that someone had actually been terminated because it took so long to restore. He explained that the inability of the IT Department to restore lost data in a timely manner was now extremely visible at the CEO level and the IT department was now considered to be incompetent at the highest level within the company. He also explained he had been working late nights and it is why he fell asleep during our first meeting and why his personal life was suffering which is why he was making his grocery list during the second presentation.

Wow! That was some valuable information about the "pain" he was feeling in his current role. AND I felt much better about why he was so disengaged during my attempts to explain what we do.

I restored the original document I designed in 2004 so I could include a copy to share here. I did edit it and took out all references to what company this was, the competitors, and specific shared applications names that were needed.

Don't bother trying to read it. I just want you to see how unpolished it was.

Despite being primitive, ugly, and very simplistic, it was so much more effective than my gorgeous, fifty slides, professionally crafted presentation that the company provided to me! How crazy is THAT?! And it was surprisingly easy to do! In fact, anybody can create something like this today!

All I did was reword each of the bullets from my presentation as though my client was saying those words.

This is important:

I stopped talking about ME and made what we did about HIM!

Company Name:
Date: 2004
Because the XYZ solution is very robust, and we have a limited amount of time to demonstrate the software, please take a moment to answer the following questions so our presentation can be customized for you and your company.

1. Attendees

Name	Title	Function

2. Specific "Deleted" Concerns - What are THREE "challenges" that you are tasked with or most concerned about?

Name	Challenge #1	Challenge #2	Challenge #3
	Compliancy	No budget	With (competitors name) today

3. Please put a check mark next to one of the three options describing your current situation with back-up and restore

Would LIKE to say this	SAY this TODAY	NA, Not Important or do not know (?)	Challenge Statement
✓			Restore is a simple and visual process
	✓		Quickly and easily find and restore missing files
✓			Avoid wasteful and costly differential back-up jobs
✓			In seconds, scroll back in time to view past server state
✓			Missing files and directories are seen as conspicuous cross-hatched objects and a single click launches the restore job
✓			Reduce hardware costs by exploiting inexpensive serial ATA-devices.
	✓		Decrease backup time
✓			Ultra quick restores from disk
✓			Integrate Disk-to-Disk-to-Tape with Synthetic Full Backup to maximize benefits.
		N/A	Backup time shrinks drastically
✓			Only incremental backups are needed. (XYZ performs full back-up 1x wk)
✓			Reduce network traffic by only sending incremental data over the LAN.
✓			Restore time is optimized since restore is from the synthetic full job on disk/tape.
✓			Potentially run incremental backups forever and synthetic fulls.
✓			Avoid wasteful and costly differential back-up jobs
	✓		Create offsite tapes during your regular, nightly backups
✓			Simultaneously write to disk and tape
✓			Save time by not having to re-run backups or having to duplicate tapes during the day.
✓			The ability to backup through a single port created as a secure outbound connection.
✓			No open (inbound) ports are needed for backup
	✓		The ability to restart a job from the point of failure
		?	The ability to pause an active job midstream?
		?	Failed backup jobs over the LAN can be automatically restarted and pick-up from where they left off and not restart the job over from the beginning
	✓		Pause and restart an active job at any time for any reason
		?	Ability to restore your own data through a web browser
		?	Personalize XML-based reports
✓			Align costs with SLAs
✓			Vendor appreciates you and treats you as a valued partner

I know it's impossible to read. I was selling business continuity software. However, no need to spend any time trying to read the details in the "Statement" section because the details are not important. Just know that each statement originally started out as a bullet in a presentation proclaiming what me and my company could do for our clients; this was the same presentation during which this client fell asleep and wrote his grocery list! And yet his reaction to this approach was completely opposite of my professional presentation. Nobody was more surprised than me at this stage of my career!

The reality is that the client doesn't care about all the cosmetics if you can't get him/her engaged in the content and have an intelligent, two-way dialogue.

If the client isn't talking, the salesperson isn't learning how to help the client!

I realize that this sounds so logical and simple. However, all sales professionals know just how difficult it can be to get clients to share information. And now we know WHY – "The Fight or Flight" instinct is a powerful adversary during each sales cycle.

The secret to overcoming this response is to get them emotionally, not just intellectually, engaged.

Creating effective Visnostic Statements and asking your audience to reflect and respond is the tactical instruction that has been missing from every sales methodology book that I have read.

This Visnostic process is unique and like nothing you have ever been taught until now.

It's important to understand that this isn't a theory or hypothesis. It is a methodology that I have been utilizing for over ten years and it has worked at multiple companies with different products and services.

It is also an approach that none of my clients have ever seen another salesperson do. It is a universal technique and since nobody is doing it, it will be refreshing to your clients when you approach them with this new communication style. That is until the lessons taught in this book become normal business practices.

This process has evolved but I will help you with the basics first and then I will explain some enhancements that have been added through the years. And as I demonstrated earlier, it doesn't have to be pretty to be effective.

About halfway through the list of my Visnostic Statements, he pushed his plate of food aside and he commented that he assumed my company could do all this or we wouldn't be going through this exercise. I said that was correct. He then asked me why the heck I didn't tell him this before now!

I looked him straight in the eyes and told him that this is the presentation that I gave him TWICE! **He laughed and said none of it even sounded familiar to him.**

This is when I realized that marketing content relies too heavily on clients' abilities to translate and interpret the actual benefits.

This new way of presenting the same information was allowing me to guide him through the thought process by eliminating the translation requirement. The result was that instead of dumping everything I could do for my client in a presentation and depending on him to translate, I was able to guide him to his own conclusion.

I also noticed that I talked a lot less and the client talked a lot more. In fact, I noticed how passionately the client started opening up to me! This was an incredible thing to witness! I NEVER got this type of reaction during a presentation!

The client came to his own conclusion versus me telling him what to think. When it is his or her idea, they will become more receptive.

He then asked if I could send him an electronic version of this new document, including his responses, by close of business that same day! I said of course!

I left the meeting and typed it all up, along with some of his commentary, which I had written on the back of this paper. He called me the next day with questions. He confessed that he edited the document and was presenting it to the CEO as his own research with a recommendation to go with us to fix specific problems that would address the restoration delays the CEO had witnessed.

Within a month of this lunch, the deal closed and it made my number for the entire year. This was a client that had no budget and obviously no interest in my presentation because **his mind was on his own problems, not what my company had to say about our company.** Aren't most clients having this same experience when we take their valuable time?

Salespeople talk way too much about their company and what they can do. Companies need their marketing departments to address this immediately! I can honestly say that nobody has ever bought from me because of the stock prices, our acquisitions, or the company strategy. **They buy because of the positive way their business will be impacted.** And salespeople don't talk enough about this because we are too busy bragging about our company. I hope as people from both sales and marketing read the Visnostic books, they see their messaging from a completely different perspective so it can be changed!

How can you fix something that you didn't realize was broken?

My content was exactly the same. The only difference was the way in which the content was communicated.

This was when I realized that HOW you articulate your message is more important than the actual content!

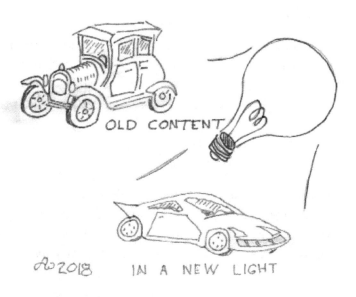

OLD CONTENT

IN A NEW LIGHT

A&2018

I felt like I had just invented the light bulb with this new approach! "No" means "Try Harder" or in this case, "No" meant that I needed to try something different.

Salespeople are going to love this book. But it's really MARKETING that needs to read it; they will become Heroes once they translate VENDOR-speak into CLIENT-speak!

Dear Marketing Team – We need your expertise to fix our messaging!!! If you are in sales, please be sure to get another copy for your favorite marketing executive!

The story about this sleepy and hungry client happened over 10 years ago and I have successfully used this approach at both big companies and small companies. I was never sure why this worked or what to call it. But as I read Mike Bosworth's most recent book, *What Great Salespeople Do*, I finally understood that this wasn't just dumb luck; there is some heavy-duty science behind it. Today, we call it Neuroscience. And it's powerful because it works!

Since 2004, I have been converting presentation bullets into this format and taking this approach with my clients with huge success. This methodology has even evolved into something more powerful. Today, when a client responds with "I can do or say this today," I now ask him to grade himself with a one through five rating system.

The scoring goes like this; if the client gives himself a one, that means they can do it but they have a lot of room for improvement. If the client scores himself a five, it means that he can do it today and he views it as perfect. And you will discover that very few people feel comfortable giving themselves a perfect score. And that is a great example of the power behind this approach.

**Once you get your clients to visualize
their current situation and then
admit that it's not perfect,
they will be more receptive to hearing what you can
do to help them achieve a better score!**

CHAPTER TWO
VISNOSTICS AND NEUROSCIENCE
Fun facts about how your brain works

Now that you know the history of Visualization Diagnostic Statements as well as some of its evolution over the past decade, let's review some basic neuroscience that you will soon observe first hand. I am confident that each reader will be amazed to find this part of the book to be enlightening and fun.

Pavlov's Theory is a famous learning procedure that involved pairing a stimulus with a conditioned response. Pavlov would ring a bell and feed his dogs a steak. Eventually, the sound of a bell would make his dogs salivate. Sadly, salespeople know all too well that bad experiences with salespeople in the past have created a NEGATIVE conditioned response towards most sales efforts. Which is where the "Fight of Flight" comes into play. In other words, salespeople are "guilty until proven innocent" by potential clients. Now imagine how cool it would be if you could find a way to trigger a POSITVE response in place of the "fight or flight" instinct! **Visnostics can do this by triggering a release of serotonin!** More on that later in this chapter.

The Science of Visnostics

Neuroscience is not just beneficial during a sales process; it is also useful in all the relationships in your life. But the value I want to provide to each reader is a detailed description of specific ways you can take the science described, convert what marketing has already created for you, and go **deliver the message in a way that your clients want and need you to deliver it! I call this "CLIENT SPEAK."**

Asking Questions Can Be Tricky – Proceed with Caution

Basic sales training will teach you to avoid closed-ended questions but sales training never explains WHY. The chemistry in your brain reacts very differently when asked a question requiring a yes or no answer than when it is asked a question that forces a visualization to occur. An example would be:

Closed-Ended Question – 'Is your car blue?'
A non-emotional cognitive/cerebral response is triggered.

Visualization Question – 'What color is your car?'
A visualization is triggered as they see their car in their thoughts, which will cause a much more emotional response.

Rapport is established during emotional responses, not cerebral ones. It is much easier to resist any decision making when emotions are not engaged.

Did you know that the second question momentarily hijacked your thought process and focused it entirely on your car? This is an automatic response. To see this in action, be sure and do the first exercise. As you read this book, it's designed to help build your own confidence and belief in the power of the science behind Visnostics. This is why the exercises exist.

A closed-ended question requires a cerebral response and a visualization question triggers a more emotional response. As sales or marketing professionals, we have been taught that people make emotional decisions much easier than a cerebral one. Emotions create a sense of urgency and a cerebral one can take you down a lengthy sales cycle resulting in the dreaded analysis paralysis.

I will review fundamental principles that you probably already know. However, what is very different with Visnostics is you will learn how to trigger powerful chemicals in the brain that will bond you with your audience like nothing you have ever experienced in the past!

When done correctly, you won't be asking a question; you will be making a statement.

Visnostic Statements force the brain to work harder to respond. This process hijacks the brain and becomes one of the most powerful and profound emotional interactions you can have with another human being during a sales process.

I've worked with several Neuroscientists to ensure accuracy with this content and I have been told my books simplify a very complex subject so everybody can understand it.

While many sales training programs focus on the cognitive and emotional aspects of the selling process, Visnostics have brought the power of the meta-cognitive to the world of sales training.

What is meta-cognitive? Metacognition refers to our awareness of and ability to regulate our own thinking. Metacognition might be the self-awareness you have around memorization. When you acknowledge that you have difficulty remembering people's names in social situations, you are engaging your metacognitive understanding of yourself.

Now imagine triggering the metacognitive awareness in your clients! Instead of relying on them to translate your features and functions into how they will benefit, you will guide them through the translation process!

I highlighted that paragraph you just read because you will want to come back to it again after you read this entire book. I realize that all this makes very little sense to you right now but as you go through the first few chapters of this book, you will gradually comprehend the power of **VIS**ualization Diag**NOSTIC** STATEMENTS™ versus questions.

By using Visnostic Statements, you will be able to bring the client's wants and wishes to the surface thus avoiding miscommunication. Furthermore, you will now have the power to get the client emotionally engaged within those critical first few seconds!

While this chapter was being written, I was a guest on a very popular sales podcast. First of all, I loved the interview and was honored to be his guest. (I also have provided links to the replays in the Appendix for your convenience.) But I was mortified when I saw that he named the podcast something like "*Use this type of QUESTION to win deals!*" **VISNOSTIC STATEMENTS ARE NOT QUESTIONS!!!!!** As I listened to the recording, I realized that he actually edited out all of my comments about how questions can trigger the dreaded "Fight of Flight" instinct that you will learn about shortly. So it was no surprise that his commentary after my interview focused on selling his training around questioning

Despite what you may have been taught, questioning isn't the Holy Grail to understanding client needs. But questions are also impossible to avoid completely. Visnostics will help your clients get in the right frame of mind to receive your questions in a more positive way. Again, you will understand this more as you read the next two chapters.

Consultative Selling was all the rage in the early 2000's and I took about a dozen different classes on how to ask questions to qualify my clients' needs. However, when I was attempting to execute the questioning principles, I could FEEL my clients getting annoyed. Think about this – when you are on the phone with a support person, they will usually ask you to take a short survey after the call. Do you actually take the time to do them? I worked for a Customer Experience Company and I can tell you that the surveys are rarely done.

Have you ever walked through a mall and someone with a clipboard tried to get you to take a quick survey? Are you excited to do it? Personally, I want to chew a body part off to escape. This desire to resist surveys is also triggered when we blast our clients with a barrage of questions. There is both an art and a science to asking questions without triggering a negative reaction.

Visnostics will teach you about the natural instincts we all have around "Fight or Flight." Because questioning will absolutely trigger these resistance responses, Visnostic Statements are a better way to get the answers you need without actually asking questions!! And your clients will appreciate this new approach because things that are new and different are often very refreshing.

What if you could learn a communication style that would release serotonin in your client's brain versus the Fight or Flight response as you spoke?

This is what Wikipedia says about serotonin - *As a neurotransmitter, serotonin helps to relay messages from one area of the brain to another. ... This includes brain cells related to mood, sexual desire and function, appetite, sleep, memory and learning, temperature regulation, and some social behavior.*

The power in triggering serotonin in your clients' brains is very similar to Pavlov's Dog. Just as Pavlov conditioned a dog to salivate every time he rang a bell; your clients will relate good feelings when they think of YOU.

I've had people try and tell me that there is no way that Visnostics will work until AFTER you establish rapport. You know what? It amazes me how many people make bold statements like that before they even attempt to do what they say won't work! Visnostics are actually THE BEST WAY I know to establish rapport!

Once you trigger those positive feelings, your clients will view you as the bell in Pavlov's theory. **YOU will actually stimulate positive responses!**

Triggering the release of serotonin is an incredible way to establish respect, rapport, and credibility instantly!

You will have your first experience executing three neuroscience exercises in Chapter Three. Some of the exercises will go extremely well while others will have some challenges and may not even work at all. But don't be discouraged.

Activities before and during the learning process will increase your retention of the content. After you read the entire book, go back and retry the exercises to see how much you have improved. It will be a great opportunity to see your progress while you evaluate your understanding of this new approach.

Practice of these principles while doing the exercises will also build your confidence so you are properly prepared to execute with your clients. These exercises are my attempt at simulating a multi-decade successful sales career. For you to have a similar passion that I do for how well this works, you will need to experience it first-hand.

There are so many books out today about neuroscience, which is basically a cool new buzzword for psychology. One of the points I read recently about neuroscience is to engage with your clients as soon as possible, which is why there are so many stories and exercises for the reader.

Repetition is also done strategically so you retain this knowledge.

The Best Visuals are NOT Static!

It's difficult to write an **engaging** book with just static visuals. Which is why I am providing numerous links to videos throughout the book. You will do your brain a great service when you take breaks to watch some videos and see movement.

Have you noticed the popular "doodle" videos that show a hand "drawing" company messages on a virtual whiteboard? These video messaging companies are booming today because our brains prefer visuals and we prefer visuals that MOVE. I have caught myself watching the same videos over and over again because they can be quite hypnotic when done correctly. Here is a pretty good article about the science behind our preferences towards videos –

5 Scientific Reasons Why Video Is Better
https://go.yumyumvideos.com/blog/5-scientific-reasons-why-online-video-engages-your-audience

The Power of THREEs

3 CANDLES   3 MICE

3 PEAKS

fw 2018

"The Power of Threes," also knows as "The Rule of Threes," has become a hot topic recently. Have you seen this new commercial by GMC? It starts off talking about "The Rule of Threes." https://www.youtube.com/watch?v=SY23zi1u_3U

I attended a leadership conference for women recently that taught the audience that the male brain prefers to have selections in groups of threes. To prove her point, the speaker showed us advertisements for three different tires. The speaker also told us that men prefer three colors of pants in their wardrobe: black, khaki, and blue. She supported these claims by having the only six men in the audience come on stage and she was correct; they all had on those colors of pants. These two simple new things I learned, helped validate why what I am about to share with you really does work and it works well!

The purpose of this story is to help you understand why I have three exercises for you to do and why you will see other topics in this book developed in sets of three.

And more importantly –
Why Visnostic Statements MUST Have THREE Options For Your Clients To Consider!

Per the facts mentioned above, at least fifty percent of our population prefers choices in threes or odd numbers. But I actually think the percentage is much higher.

3 CANDLES

The points made about men's brains reminded me of a woman's decorating class that taught that we think we want symmetrical settings, but our brain actually prefers things in uneven numbers.

Therefore, it can be concluded that these preferences for groupings in sets of three are not just applicable to men.

As you conduct Visnostic discussion, you will be tempted to take short cuts or simplify by just offering ONE of the THREE selections to your clients but if you do that, you will be converting a statement into a question! AND you will be eliminating the POWER OF THREES! Do NOT do that!

You will make your Visnostic STATEMENT (speaking from the Client's perspective/First Person) and ask them to select one of three responses:

1. **I can say this today. (If so, score yourself 1-5 with 5 being perfect)**
2. **I WISH I could say this today.**
3. **It's not important, I don't know, or not applicable.**

Visnostic Discussions are NOT Questions! Questions are risky and can trigger the "Fight or Flight" instinct that we all have.

People that provide training about how to ask questions will argue against his point so let me give a few examples that support this claim —

- Do you get excited and eager when you receive a call from someone asking you to spend just a few minutes as they conduct a survey?
- Do you eagerly wait after a support call so you can respond to the survey about your satisfaction with the call?
- Do you get excited when someone with a clipboard approaches you to ask you a few questions?

If you answer yes to any of these examples, you are an anomaly. For most people, questioning is an annoyance. When somebody starts asking us questions, we instinctively suspect that their objective or agenda is sketchy which is why we become guarded and even a bit defensive.

We also need to know what is in it for US? If you write your statements correctly, your first three words will clearly explain what is in it for your audience because you will start with the **WHY/RESULTS** and **HOW/TIMELINE** we covered in the

Introduction. If you are one of those readers that skips Forewords and Introductions, I highly recommend you go back and read them or you will be lost during the next few chapters.

For more information on questions, please look in the Appendix; you will find additional articles that will support the points I make about Visnostic Statements and why statements are much more impactful than questions. But the reality is that we will never eliminate the need for SOME questions as we interact with others.

Fight or Flight or Freeze

I've already mentioned "Fight or Flight" multiple times but now I'm going to dive a little deeper into the very important neuroscience behind it.

There are a few fundamental human instincts to keep in mind as you read the next few chapters. First of all, "fight or flight" is a real thing that haunts salespeople. Humans have a natural instinct to put up walls, become defensive, or flee when someone is trying to sell to them, ask them for money, or persuade them.

You still don't believe this?

- When you see a sales call on your caller ID, do you enthusiastically answer your phone?

- When you answer the phone and it is a charity or salesperson, do you hang-up on them?

- Do you interrupt and tell them that you don't have time to talk?

- When you walk into a store, and a salesperson asks if they can help you, do you attempt to brush them off by telling them that you are just looking?

What other tactics do you use to avoid listening to them pitch to you? Your responses were probably very much like the responses you have towards SURVEYS (i.e. QUESTIONS)!

As you read that there will be exercises, do you recall how that made you feel? Even if it occurred in your subconscious, I bet that you already decided and JUSTIFIED why you don't need to do the exercises. Am I right? Humans are complex but we can be incredibly predictable as well.

Because I have been selling my entire career, you would think that I would be more receptive and patient with salespeople. However, I am far from it. I even took the time to add all of my numbers to the United States Do Not Call Registry.

Do Not Call

The **Do Not Call Registry** accepts registrations from both cell phones and land lines. To **register** by telephone, **call** 1-888-382-1222 (TTY: 1-866-290-4236). You must **call** from the phone number that you want to **register**. To **register** online (**donotcall**.gov), you **will** have to respond to a confirmation email.

Sadly, it hasn't helped at all which has intensified my resentment of that disruption in my life. Salespeople are annoying because our brains are wired to flee from persuasive scenarios. Therefore, people that force us to do things that are unnatural are difficult to trust.

Visnostics is how to sell without getting the negative reaction that naturally occurs towards sales efforts.

With the "Fight or Flight" instinct in mind, please inform your participant that you are doing an experiment from a book you are reading. Then ask if they would please **help** you by participating by responding to a few statements.

Remember that most people enjoy an opportunity to help as long as there isn't a catch or a hidden agenda.

I am passionate about Visnostics but it's taken me over 20 years to build a testimony and belief in their effectiveness. Exercises are the only way I know to simulate a virtual experience so each reader can build his or her own testimony. If you are like me, you must believe in something in order to actually go out and EXECUTE!

Fight your Flight instincts and do these exercises!

CHAPTER THREE
TRANSLATION CHALLENGES

There are at least two types of translations that take place during a sales cycle. Salespeople are trying to **map** their products and services to the pain and needs of the client and the client is trying to **interpret** how the features and functions of the vendor's offering will make his or her world better.

This may sound simple and logical. However, the potential for a translation error is extremely high. And while this is a universal issue, we continue to handle it poorly because we ignore that the problem even exists!

Just like the "roast story" we have been doing this wrong for so long that it's become "normal."

Therefore, we don't even question the way we do it today; marketing produces collateral and various other messaging filled with "features and functions" and expects that our clients will do all the heavy lifting and translate those F&F into why they care. HUGE MISTAKE!

Sales AND Marketing
need to take
the translation risks
out of the sales cycle.

Painting a clear vision with your audience is an important step in the communication process. Yet this topic is omitted in most books because I don't think many people know an easy way to address the challenge.

The first step in this translation process is to ensure sales is speaking the same language as the client. This is accomplished through a series of Visnostic Statements that paint a VISION or VISUALIZATION for the client to validate or clarify.

What does Visualization mean to you? Visualization is often described using several words like mapping, conversion, translation, interpretation, and envisioning. What if your vision is different than what your client is envisioning?

Translating "what you do" into "why your audience should care" is hard work as well as risky. If ineffective, it can lead to a total disconnect between sales and the client. This communication breakdown is the biggest reason for lost sales and lost clients.

To add to this communication challenge, marketing often uses **subjective** words in their attempts to paint a vision for the clients. Words and phrases such as "world class" "best of breed," "considerable," "extensive," "immediate," or "quickly" can cause serious miscommunication between you and your client.

In fact, you could be setting yourself up for a future dissatisfied client because their expectations may be completely out of sync with the reality of your deliverable.

In addition, marketing tends to use their own trademarked words, slang, acronyms, and industry jargon which are also extremely confusing and dangerous during the communication process with clients.

Visnostics will help you translate your client's vision so you can ACCURATELY map your offering to their specific needs!

In fact, Visualization Diagnostic (Visnostic) Statements will flush out these important facts before you ever even present to your client!

I'm guessing that most of what I just explained makes no sense to you right now so I am going to TRANSLATE these points by telling another story. Once you read the story, you may want to re-read the first few pages of Chapter Three to see if they make more sense.

A Different Type of Christmas Story

One of my more painful losses was due to a translation mistake on my part. My client and I had two very different visions of what my company could do for them.

There was a time when companies needed to migrate data from one device to another device. To do this, companies had to bring down production to do a migration and holidays were a common time to do this due to low activity. I sold software that allowed companies to do this migration while production was live. Needless to say, this was a pretty easy sale.

I was in Dallas at a major retailers headquarters and I had already done a lot of homework. One of the men was a technical influencer and he mentioned to me that he hadn't been home with his family on Christmas Day in years. He explained that he would watch his children open their gifts and then head to the office for the rest of the day. I couldn't wait to give him the good news! He would never miss Christmas with his family ever again!

I thought I nailed the presentation! So you can imagine my shock at how quickly I was told that I would not be winning their business. I went back to their office to find out what I did wrong. To my surprise, the man that told me about working Christmas Day admitted that he was the one that killed the deal.

His reason was very simple. He relied very heavily on the triple pay he got on Christmas Day to buy the gifts for his family each year. Therefore, he viewed our services as a threat, not a benefit. **When he told me that he hadn't been home in years, I interpreted that as a bad thing**. I found out too late that he actually depended on it. In addition, there were additional days he got extra pay that my company and I would also eliminate. In other words, my offering hurt him and his family personally! **This was a very painful lesson about the risk involved when translating sales benefits to client benefits.** I would have bet my commission check that he viewed me as his HEROINE, not his VILLAIN!

A great Visnostic Statement for this would have been, "I will never have to work on weekends or holidays ever again!" His reply would have been "Not important, not applicable, or I don't know" which would have been a huge indicator for me to get clarification from the client BEFORE I went in with guns-a-blazing about how he would get to spend Christmas with his family!

EXERCISE #1
The Power of Visualization for Translating

This is very simple to do and it works every single time!

In 2007, I was part of a transformation team that toured the country teaching "Order Takers" how to be "Hunters." I began my presentation with a little exercise that I want you to try before you read any further.

I don't know where you are right now. You may be on a plane, or reading this in bed before you go to sleep, or on a lunch break. It doesn't matter where you are right now; what matters is that you have an innocent bystander that you can nab and ask him or her to participate in an exercise that will take less than 15 seconds.

If you are alone, DO NOT be tempted to pick up the phone to call someone because it is important that you watch the participant's eyes. After you explain this is an experiment,

just say these simple words –

"I am going to say a word and I need you to tell me the first VISUAL that pops into your head. What is the first thing you SEE when you hear this word…."

(Pause) Are you ready? (Pause)
"MONEY"

Be sure to carefully watch the eyes.

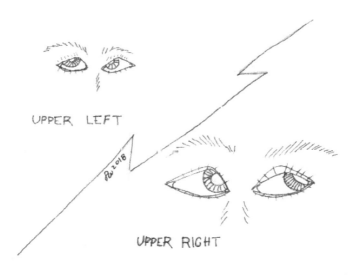

The eyes will move rather fast so if you blink, you may miss it. Often, you will see them look up to the right or up to the left. As sales professionals, we should know the basics of body language and this means they are thinking and visualizing something.

Ask them to be as detailed as possible when describing what they see. It's incredible how fast our minds visualize memories. Please send me an email describing what they say to you to this email address – **money@dynaexec.com**.

I encourage you to do this exercise with multiple people so you can see for yourself how such a simple and universal word – really ISN'T so universal!

It is important that you follow these instructions because emailing me a description of what happened will help reinforce what you saw and learned. Those that skip this step will not improve as much as those that take time to reflect, envision, and document the observations of this exercise.

Lessons Learned From Exercise #1

There are so many lessons to be learned by doing this exercise. This exercise does a terrific job demonstrating how a simple word can be translated HUNDREDS of different ways! It's actually amazing we can properly communicate at all!

First of all – Look at yourself. When I first discussed this exercise with various neuroscientists, I predicted 10% of the readers would email me as instructed. The neuroscientists laughed at me and said it would be MUCH lower. They are correct. Less than ten people have emailed me out of hundreds of readers in the past six months. So if you are reading this and you realize you were in the majority, ask yourself why you ignored the instructions even after all the benefits were laid out for you. Now ask yourself why you think your customers will behave differently when you call or email asking for a meeting. Interesting. Right?

Another lesson is that our minds visualize things extremely fast when it is something to which we can relate.

A third lesson is that different minds process data differently. I did this exercise during a recent podcast and I laughed at how fast Dr. Pelè blurted out, "ME!" This is normal because I often get short and fast answers during this exercise but every once in a while, a person will describe what sounds like a movie!

Sometimes when I ask what a person visualizes, they describe FEELINGS instead of what they SEE. This response is very unusual but the responses are, by far, the most passionate and lengthy descriptions.

I was with a lady that I have hired three different times. She is the best salesperson and relationship builder I have ever met. However, I consistently had challenges keeping her focused. I always assumed it was because she has been diagnosed with ADD.

As we reviewed the draft of this book together, I became very aware that her brain moves faster and she envisions many more details than most people. What she described to me when she heard the word "Money" was extremely emotional and thorough. She described money as being a source of freedom and then gave me multiple examples. The word triggered more emotions from her than any other person I have ever encountered. Her explanation went on for over ten minutes and her eyes were darting in every direction.

I realized that not only did I get an understanding of how she views the word "money,' I also got an education on how different her thought process is compared to other people that have done this exercise with me. I was seeing first-hand how difficult it is for a person with such an active brain to be focused on one thing at a time.

I realized that I needed to be aware of how her brain processes information and visualizes conversations so I can understand how I might want to adjust my own communication style with her. This will be enlightening as you get to know new clients as well. As she was talking, I wondered how many brains like hers have been diagnosed as having ADD when in reality their brains are much more active than other brains. To me, what I was witnessing was a gift or talent versus a handicap or disability as ADD is often viewed.

A few weeks later, I did this same exercise with a relative and she said she has so many negative feelings around the word money. She also went into great detail about the bad feelings that surfaced when she heard this word.

Words can trigger unexpected emotional responses.

Both of these ladies described **feelings** when they heard the word versus an **image**. One responded positively emotionally and the other responded negatively. The word was the same but the responses and perceptions were complete opposites.

Why does this matter? Those of you that watched the video I recommended in the Introduction will know exactly why this is important to understand. Those that skipped the video might want to stop reading and go watch it right now. Here it is again so you don't have to go looking for it:
"You are Who You Are, Because of Where You Were, When"
https://www.youtube.com/watch?v=_aY163kwIW4

When you are presenting, you probably assume that your audience comprehends your message the way you intend it to be received. But how can you determine if you are accomplishing this goal? How do you determine how your client is processing information? Those that visualize a movie may have a more challenging time keeping up during a fast-paced presentation. Others may zone out because they feel your content and pace are much too slow. These reactions may cause you to lose important points with some members of your audience.

What if I told you that Visnostic Statements will ensure that your clients communicate their interpretation of your messaging? This will enable you to avoid miscommunication from occurring.

Getting your audience to visualize and articulate their current situation is the most impactful way to get them emotionally engaged in your conversation. Their comments will also validate their comprehension of the points you are making.

During this money exercise, the more details your participant gives you, the more emotional engagement you will observe. The eyes will reveal additional emotions and you can observe the magnitude of the visualizations taking place in their mind. Try and do this exercise with several people and compare how many different types of responses you observe.

Now let's discuss why most people will resist following the instructions around this exercise.

While writing and sharing with a test group, not one person followed the instructions or shared their experience with me via email as requested. This in itself is proof that when someone feels they are being coerced or persuaded to do something, the natural instinct is to rebel and flee. It was simply too much work for the reader.

So why do we expect a different response from our clients? Translating is hard work. That makes it very risky for sales because it can lead to misinterpretations by your clients.

The more work you do for the client, the more you will be perceived as adding value and the more receptive your client will be to your message.

fw 2018

I did the money exercise with one of my favorite recruiters and she told me that she saw an orange.

Because this was the first time I had ever heard that response, I asked her to elaborate on why she saw an orange. She explained that money buys her food and she loves oranges. So this conversation with my recruiter is even more evidence of how one single word can mean so many different things to many different people. As salespeople, one of our biggest challenges is to understand how our audience is interpreting our words.

Words translate differently because we each have different experiences. One single word can mean different things triggering completely different emotions within each person.

I recall many conversations I have had with clients over the years where we had communication challenges. Often, their interpretations of industry terms such as "the cloud" or "implementation" were very different than my company or mine.

When I wrote my first book, I decided I wanted to leverage a Publisher. I learned quickly that my vision of the role a Publisher would play in my life was very different than the vision my Publisher had. This different expectation of what a Publisher is has caused a great deal of disappointment for both of us.

Try and think of a communication breakdown you've had recently due to different interpretations of what words meant. In fact, any married person should have LOTS of stories!

As I described in an earlier story, even working on Christmas Day can have different perspectives and produce different emotional responses. Understanding your client's unique visualizations will help you exceed, versus falling short of, their expectations.

Wouldn't it be cool if you could get into your clients' heads? Once you are aware of their visualizations, you won't make the mistake of focusing on YOUR visions by accident as I did in my previous Christmas Day Story.

Look at this cartoon. What does it mean? You'll do this again at the end of the book and compare how much you've grown.

Visnostic Statements flush out your clients' visualizations thus reducing the risk of communication misinterpretations, disappointments, disconnects, or breakdowns.

Too many times, the client's expectations do not match the salesperson's interpretations of those expectations.

This communication breakdown is why this book is so important.

I have conducted the "Money Exercise" hundreds of times since 2007. Most people say they see physical items such as bags of money, coins, stacks of currency, and bags of gold. Others see symbols like a $ dollar, € Euro, ¥ Yen, or £ Pound. Some of the more creative and humorous responses I have heard are things like the alimony check I write each month, my mortgage payment, bills, my tuition payment, my home, my children, my spouse, my parents...the list goes on and on.

I invited people on LinkedIn to participate in this exercise; with the promised they would be included in this book. Here are some of those responses:

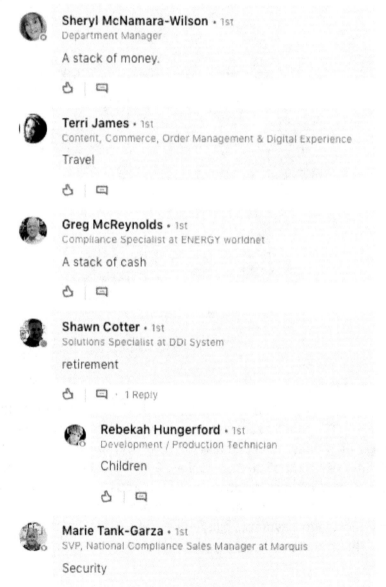

Sheryl McNamara-Wilson · 1st
Department Manager

A stack of money.

Terri James · 1st
Content, Commerce, Order Management & Digital Experience

Travel

Greg McReynolds · 1st
Compliance Specialist at ENERGY worldnet

A stack of cash

Shawn Cotter · 1st
Solutions Specialist at DDI System

retirement

· 1 Reply

Rebekah Hungerford · 1st
Development / Production Technician

Children

Marie Tank-Garza · 1st
SVP, National Compliance Sales Manager at Marquis

Security

It actually boggles my mind when I think about how a simple and popular word like "money" can mean so many different things to so many different people! **THIS IS A MAJOR POINT OF THIS BOOK!**

But the main lesson learned in Exercise #1 may shock many readers because **there are no right or wrong answers when asked to describe what is visualized when hearing the word** *MONEY*. **This exercise demonstrated that each person will TRANSLATE or convert those letters into something meaningful that is unique to him or her.**

Therefore, **this exercise proves that presenting WHAT your company does and WHY it does it, is NOT effective and is high risk. There is a high probability that your client's may not translate your words as you intended!**

The biggest surprise in this exercise is not what people say in response. It is what they DON'T say that should make every single reader change the way in which he or she communicates.

Here is the part of Exercise #1 that should make those light bulbs start going off for many readers:

DRUM ROLL

Despite receiving hundreds of different responses, not one single person has **EVER** said they saw a slide with a bullet and the **LETTERS...**

M

O

N

E

Y

We simply do not visualize letters or words. In fact, our brains are a lot like a computer. Computers convert binary code full of 1's and 0's into something on the screen that we can comprehend. **Our brains turn letters into words, and words into visuals!**

_____

EXERCISE #2
The Pain of Translation

Below is a sentence written in binary code. You can search online for "binary code translator" and type these numbers into it and it will automatically translate it for you. Email the translation to money@dynaexec.com.

Less than 1% of you will be curious enough to figure out how to translate it. That means 99% of you will engage your flight instinct to justify avoiding that effort. In fact, despite hundreds of books sold, less than 10 people have done this exercise and there is a very important message in this binary code!

**01010000 01100101 01101111 01110000 01101100
01100101 00100000 01100001 01110110 01101111
01101001 01100100 00100000 01110100 01110010
01100001 01101110 01110011 01101100 01100001
01110100 01101001 01101111 01101110 00100001**

Our brains do the same thing when they convert letters to physical things that we can comprehend. Just as computers translate zeros and ones into letters and symbols, salespeople need to translate letters and words into the PROPER visualization for our clients! You may want to re-read this paragraph multiple times to retain this major point!!!

So my questions to each reader are:

WHY DO WE KEEP PRESENTING SLIDES LOADED WITH BULLETS AND LETTERS?

———

WHY DO WEBSITES HAVE MORE WORDS THAN GRAPHICS?

———

WHY DO THE GRAPHICS NOT EVEN MATCH THE MESSAGE?

———

WHY ARE MOST BUSINESS BOOKS FULL OF WORDS YET VERY FEW PICTURES?

———

WHY CREATE ANY MARKETING MATERIALS LOADED WITH PICTURES THAT HAVE ZERO TO DO WITH THE TOPIC?

———

WHY IS INSTRAGRAM SO POPULAR WHEN IT'S MOSTLY JUST PHOTOS AND GRAPHICS?

Could this be how your competitors beat you? Could they be doing a better job translating their offerings into "client-speak?" Let's make YOU the competitor that is winning!

I was conducting a workshop last week and I was told about an $80 million client that was lost to a competitor last year. The client's decision to make the change was because the competitor identified something they could do that was perceived as unattainable with the current provider.

The sad part of this story is that the incumbent vendor COULD do the same service but the client was unable to translate the confusing features and functions, acronyms, fancy product names, buzz words, and jargon adequately. This was a very costly translation error that we all want to avoid. But how do we address this? Marketing, please read this carefully: **All those words you invent and all those fluffy words that sound so good are NOT helping clients understand your message!**

To those of you that skipped Exercise #2:

Your Fight or Flight was triggered. Why are you surprised when you get the same avoidance from a client that you just dumped a folder full of documents such as a presentation, a long email, a bunch of URLs, a brochure, acronyms, industry jargon, or some other sort of marketing collateral that you sincerely thought/hoped would trigger buying behaviors?

Why do we have slides that have pretty backgrounds versus backgrounds that help the audience retain the content? Why are we surprised when we don't get a response? Do you send emails hoping to get meetings? Do YOU read your SPAM or junk mail? Is selling to you via email effective? If not, why are you doing the same things to your clients? Does it feel good to tell yourself that you made some sort of effort? Wouldn't you feel better if these efforts produced better RESULTS?

Marketing teams get excited when they see a 3%-5% response from marketing campaigns. This is another "roast story" moment! Why is that acceptable? What if we could improve those percentages by doing things differently?

"Visnostic Statements will increase your success significantly because they avoid triggering this avoidance response.

For the <1% of you that actually did translate the binary numbers, was this translation painful? Just as computers convert 0s and 1s into letters for us to understand, words in a brochure or slide must be translated by our clients for them to envision how the words relate to their lives.

As a READER, you are attempting to translate what you are reading right now into ways you will use this. As a WRITER, I am trying to translate for you! It's not easy or everybody would be doing it!

When we describe our companies offerings to potential clients, they are already having to translate words into why they care. Why are we throwing features and functions at them as well? By doing this, we are adding another level of unnecessary translation!

Earlier, I mentioned that when I presented about the "cloud" and "implementation" services my company provided, I noticed a lot of confusion in the audience. Those two words have meant different things to almost every single client I have spoken with. Reflecting back, none of my messaging had any graphics that would have clarified what I meant for the audience. This would have helped avoid quite a bit of the misunderstandings that took place.

Recently, a Fortune 50 company was presenting to me and I was distracted by the graphics used because I couldn't understand how they tied to the presentation. I later realized that their presentation was a corporate standardized "style" that everyone had to use but the background and graphics had nothing to do with the content of the presentation I was hearing. The slides were gorgeous; marketing did a great job creating company standard fonts, colors, graphics, backgrounds, and other cosmetics but marketing really didn't understand the confusion these templates would cause during presentations because they are creating things without understanding the various ways in which these mandatory templates were actually used.

Conversion is necessary for true comprehension. Yet, how many clients make the time to go through this process? I suspect that the numbers are very low. When we load decks or websites up with bullets and words, we force our clients to translate those words and letters into something meaningful in their lives. Guess what? The chances of that happening are about the same percentages of those that followed instructions in Exercise #2.

Many readers will even go to the Appendix looking for the translated answer, which is why you won't find it. What is stronger in you; your flight instinct or curiosity? Chances are that your flight is stronger. So why expect a different response from your clients?

If this somewhat simple exercise made you work too hard and your "flight" instinct was activated, why are you doing this to your clients with your websites, brochures, and presentations? Sales and Marketing need to work TOGETHER to fix this ASAP!!

Visnostic Statements eliminate this translation step, which is why your clients will engage and comprehend much faster.

EXERCISE #3
Creating Your First Visnostic Statements

This exercise will get you prepared for the next chapter. You are about to see a photo of a Treo Cell Phone. It was one of the first smart devices for sale yet the company is no longer in business. The picture represents how they sold their phone. Keep in mind, this was during a time when most people still had separate devices for storing client contact information, cameras, and calendars, just to name a few.

Just fifteen years ago, cell phones were only used to make calls and maybe do some very primitive texting.

If you saw an advertisement with these features and functions listed, how would you translate this data? How would this fancy phone make your life better?

You have a huge advantage over the original consumers reading this advertisement because you can relate to it already. But imagine if you had never seen a cell phone that did anything beyond making a call! Imagine a time when texting meant you had to push the #2 key three times to type a letter C!

NEW One-touch shortcut to Wi-Fi

Volume buttons

Customizable side button

Start
Phone/Talk
One-touch shortcut to Calendar

Ringer on/off switch
Stylus
Camera (on back)
Speakerphone (on back)
NEW 320x320 color touchscreen
Multi-function power/end function
One-touch shortcut to email Inbox
5-way navigator
MicroUSB connector

So try and imagine it is 2002 and you saw this ad. Translate and convert at least EIGHT of these features into how you would use it. How could this phone make your life better? What would you be able to do differently with this smart device that you couldn't do with a typical cell phone?

The next chapter will unveil the importance of this exercise.

1.
2.
3.
4.
5.
6.
7.
8.

CHAPTER FOUR
VENDOR-SPEAK VERSUS CLIENT-SPEAK

C hapter Three's purpose was to help you understand the struggles we all have with translation and the powerful influence the "Fight or Flight" instinct has over our potential clients.

Chapter Four will dive deeper into the importance of translating Vendor-Speak into Client-Speak. What does this all mean? Well, because we are all different, when we hear the word MONEY, we envision different things based upon who we are and where we are in our life in that particular moment. As you can tell by all the different responses when asked what people see when they hear money, just think of all the words in your current marketing message that can also be misinterpreted.

What further complicates things is when marketing messaging focuses on features and functions instead of results, the clients are now forced to listen to those marketing words around features and functions and TRANSLATE them into why they care. The only way we can ensure that translation is as we intend it, is to do the translation for our clients. This can be extremely difficult to do unless we somehow climb inside our clients' minds and see exactly what they see. Visnostics do exactly this!

If marketing doesn't translate features and functions (vendor-speak) into results/why clients care (client-speak), that means salespeople must convert the marketing message and guide the client's vision towards real life execution. But what if your clients have figured out a better way to leverage your offerings? What if your marketing message is incomplete? What if your clients understand your offering better than YOU do?

Here is one of the most impactful stories that happened in my career and it is a perfect example of why translation is the most important topic in this book and why it is both sale's and marketing's responsibility to be experts around translation.

An Accidental Client Translation Success Story

Earlier, I described losing a sale due to a translation error regarding working during Christmas. Now I want to share a story how I **accidentally** won a sale. Thanks to a very smart client, she was able to translate my marketing message into how she would actually USE my offering.

My company sold a small amount of software to a client in hopes that the quantities of the software license would grow after they saw the value. However, nobody was using it, so I insisted on conducting an onsite training session. We were teaching them how to use the software to restore their backups.

Each student had his or her own monitor with the software running. We were in the middle of a hands on demonstration when suddenly, a woman shrieked with delight. She screamed, "You are teaching this all wrong! This is not a recovery tool, this is an application management tool and we have been looking for something like this for almost a year! " She then explained that they were about to lose a major government contract because an important application kept crashing their system and nobody could figure out what was causing it. All the vendors pointed fingers at each other. She called me over to her monitor and showed me that a hidden part of these applications was being misidentified by their virus detection system and destroyed. Now that they could see hidden files associated with all their applications, they could identify what was causing the crash and they would save their government contract.

The ability for my client to translate our training content into how it could actually be used at her company resulted in one of the fastest closes of my career. And to this day, it is also the largest commission check I have ever earned...accidentally.
The reality is that my client is the one that earned this commission! That's extremely difficult to admit.

This was a huge lesson learned as these Visualization Diagnostic Statements evolved.

My COMPANY taught me to sell the way the product was designed to work (Vendor-Speak) but my CLIENT taught me how they could actually benefit from the software (Client-Speak)!

I was fortunate that I had a client in that classroom that was able to translate our marketing message and our product training session into something meaningful to her company. Unfortunately this is extremely rare! We cannot rely on clients to do the translating. It is sales responsibility to do the work for the client.

When was the last time you reached out to your clients to understand how they use your offerings?

Clients should be your primary source for the Client-centric results that are the main part of your Visnostic Statements.

Earlier, I mentioned the WHY/RESULTS are how we should start off our conversations with potential new clients. But this is impossible to do until you gather this data! Where would YOU get this information? The answer is THE EXISTING CLIENTS! And this doesn't necessarily mean that you need to contact them directly. It's possible this work has already been done.

If you haven't read your case studies, you should start collecting the content right away. As you read them, look for RESULTS. You will use this information when we begin creating your first statements. If you don't have case studies or something that describes success stories of clients, this may actually be a red flag with your current employer.

Sadly, I have worked for companies that couldn't provide this information because the offerings were not real. I've also worked for companies that didn't document client successes because they feared the information would get into the competitors hands. This is ridiculous but it is a fear that actually exists.

Don't fail at your job because you are relying on someone else to provide these results to you. However, if you are in marketing, this is great way to win friends on the sales team if you can provide these golden nuggets.

Marketing AND Salespeople should be in front of existing clients anyway. Just as my client taught me a new way to sell my software, you may be surprised how much positive information you can learn from your existing clients. And if they are happy with your company and the results they are experiencing, they should be more than happy to share detailed results with you. They may even be willing to speak with other prospective clients as a reference for your company.

The Conversion Process

Conversion is a form of translation. Converting features and functions (Vendor-Speak) into Visualization Diagnostic Statements (Client-Speak) is the act of translating vendor centric wording into a first-person description that the client can relate.

If you could only do ONE thing unveiled so far, I hope it would be to convert your current Features and Functions into Visnostics. Because this conversion process provides dramatic and instant results, it's extremely important that you understand the significance of Exercise #3.

The Birth of Smart Devices

This is the story about the demise of one of the first smart phones and why distinguishing vendor content from client content is critical when creating successful Visnostic Statements.

Blackberry and Treo were two of the first Smart Phones released. I saw my first Treo advertisement in Fortune Magazine right after travel was horribly impacted by the tragedy of 911.

The ad mentioned that the only carrier that would offer this phone would be Sprint. The ad made such an impact on me, that I pulled the page out of my magazine and immediately contacted Sprint to get details about changing service providers. Despite having one of the best service contracts at the time, I was willing and eager to change carriers just to get this phone into my life. So the ad was effective. Right?

Actually, it was not. I was one of a small minority that looked at this ad and was able to TRANSLATE it into why I cared.

The airports were miserable immediately after the attacks on 9/11. Internet existed but it wasn't widely available and it was expensive. I couldn't find a copy of the exact ad I saw but it was very similar to this photo.

Here are some actual results from that translation and what my responses would have been in Exercise #3:

1. The ad said I could send and receive email without Internet. I translated this to mean that I could do email at the airport for the first time ever from a PHONE! I could actually be productive while waiting for delayed flights to arrive.

2. It said it had a keyboard. This meant I would no longer need to hit the #2 key three times in order to type a C!

3. It said it had a camera. This meant I didn't need to lug around my camera, charger, and accessories anymore.

4. It said I could store my client phone numbers on my phone. PalmPilot made Treo and it was one of the first phones that actually stored contacts' phone numbers in the phone. This meant that I could transfer all of my contacts from the PalmPilot I carried everywhere into my phone and not have to carry yet another device or its charger around airports anymore.

5. It showed some of the apps that were included. I noticed that there was a calendar app, which meant I could throw away my bulky and heavy day timer.

6. It said that the phone had a stylus. I admit this one stumped me. I had to do some research to figure out

why I should care about this. I uncovered that another app was for taking notes and I could use a stylus to write on the screen just like I would in a journal. This was another excuse to ditch the heavy and bulky day timer and pen.

You get the picture. Everything Treo did in their marketing was "VENDOR-SPEAK." How did your translation in Exercise #3 compare to mine? I imagine it would be different since Smart Phones are now an integral part of our culture. The point of all this is that Treo stressed the components, features, and functions of it's wonderful device. They hoped that consumers were smart enough to translate that into how it would make their lives better. I was able to do that, but they really missed out on a huge opportunity to gain and keep a much larger market share. Back in those days, a phone was a phone. Period. The concept of a device that was basically a miniature computer was really difficult for most of society to comprehend. Those of us in the technology world had an easier time understanding the vision and potential of these types of devices. However, we were a minority from the general population. Blackberry was basically marketing the same way so the consumers that DID figure out the translation then had to choose between two phones that sounded almost exactly the same.

Then came Apple's iPhone and things changed RAPIDLY because their "CLIENT-SPEAK" marketing was refreshing and embraced by the marketplace. Do you recall the original iPhone commercials? They never talked about the storage, the operating system, the applications, or any technical specs at all. They showed cool people doing cool things like listening to music, taking pictures and video, and having a great time! They showed how this new device was going to change lives for the better and people would have fun while doing it! Again, those commercials told a story; it didn't put us into a coma with all the features and functions or speeds and feeds and it worked so well that Treo no longer exists and Blackberry continues to struggle for market share.

In contrast, Apple is worth billions of dollars and almost every person reading right now has had at least one iPhone. Apples success is such a great example of what happens when you create client-centric messaging versus vendor-centric messaging in your marketing content.

Thanks to Apple's translation efforts, the majority of the population finally understood how these incredible Smart Devices could change lives for the better. Apple figured out a way to paint the vision for the clients and help them avoid that translation requirement. Treo and Blackberry were completely blindsided by Apple's unique marketing approach as Apple took market share (in what felt like) overnight.

What Great Salespeople Do taught us that decisions are made with the emotional side of our brain, not the logical side. Which side do you think is stimulated with technical details? If people make emotional buying decisions, why do we include technical details? Apple has done a brilliant job making us emotional about our Apple products.

Because of the rise and fall I observed of these two incredibly innovative companies, I became very analytical of the presentation materials of companies that I represented.

I believe that the inability to articulate a message that resonated with the general public, and the marketing of features and functions, are what led to the eventual acquisition and demise of Treo.

Overcoming the Temptation to
Kill Our Clients With Data

Therefore, when I start with a new company, one of the first things I want to see is the corporate sales presentation. I was with a Fortune 500 company that was ranked in the top 50. Surprisingly, their deck was over 180 slides of technical details! I asked my coworkers if they really subjected their client base to this deck and they confirmed that not only was accurate, it took a full day to go through the entire deck! I also want to mention that sales were in a decline and all the competitors were picking off loyal, long-term clients at an alarming rate. Any guesses why?

After several years of reviewing feature and function marketing collateral and translating them so I could create my own sales tools, I have finally created a formalized process that I conduct today as a full day translation workshop.

NOTE: During the feedback collected when this book was a draft, several reviewers pointed out that their respective industries did not use many presentation decks. What you are about to read is an analysis of a Slide Deck used for presentations. However, these same principles apply to any marketing messaging. This analysis process applies to all forms of marketing, including elevator pitches, website content, mobile device applications, brochures, infographics, videos, podcasts, or any other marketing venues or channels you use to share your business's marketing message with prospective clients.

I actually debated removing this part of the book because I suspect I lost a lot of readers during a very long "Step 1" but there are several great ideas for sales and marketing people in here that could result in increased sales. So I couldn't justify deleting all this valuable information. If you are bored, skip to Step 2 versus putting the book down. But before you make that decision, please read this story:

One of the readers that I helped recently presented to me and I recorded it. When he was done, I told him that his first seven slides were about things that clients do not care about. These slides included information on the company's history, it's recent IPO (initial public offering), board members, growth rate, executives, and more coma-inducing facts.
I pointed out that only one slide had any data that his audience would care about because only one slide had

content about client RESULTS. I suggested that he make is own slide and leverage Visnostics and those results for content.

He had mentioned that the CEO was going to be in the meeting so I asked him to find a photo of the CEO and paste it in the middle of the slide and then create bubbles (like the ones on all of my book covers) and write them "Visnosticly."

He didn't have much time because the presentation was the next day but he agreed to try this approach. Did I mention that six previous salespeople had attempted to sell to this prospective client and all of them failed?

The next day, he was so excited, he actually called me from the parking lot. He said he took my advice, created the CEO slide, converted all his bullets about what they could do, into first person statements and started each sentence with client results. He wrote them as though the CEO was saying each of them. He said he never got off that first slide! He said that the CEO actually talked more than he did!

Fifteen minutes prior to the conclusion of the meeting, my new reader asked the CEO if he wanted to finish the slides or discuss the next steps, the CEO said, "No need to show me anymore slides, we are going to move forward with you. This was the best presentation I've seen from your company. Great job and thank you for not killing me with stuff I don't care about!"

Step 1 is long but it's a critical part of the analysis process as you evaluate your existing messaging and start preparing to convert it from Vendor-Speak to Client-Speak. I hope you stick with the reading. It WILL be worth it!

Step 1 – Analyze Your Content – Transcribe & Categorize by Segmentation

The Visnostic definition of Segmentation is a breakdown of your offering. Different components of your offering will require different types of Visnostic Statements.

For example, a Hybrid Cloud solution will be segmented by software, hardware, network devices, and services. In contrast, a Real Estate office may require Visnostics that are based upon buyer interests, seller interests, a combination of both buyer and seller concerns, and the recruitment of potential agents. An auto dealership may want to segment by the model of cars, service department, driver experience, financing options, upsell features, and affordability. I'm sure I'm leaving some out but I wanted to give you enough examples to stimulate your own thought process. Don't skip segmentation because it's important when building a powerful sales tool in the last chapter.

For Step One of your content analysis, have someone give the presentation and record it. If they used a script, get an electronic copy of that, as well. It will help during the transcription and categorization process. Try and separate vendor-centric components of the presentation from the client-centric content in the presentation. **If your presentation is very feature/function or product focused, try and separate the content of what you do from how the client will use it.** Keep an eye out for buzz words, acronyms, and keep a list so you identify them.

The main things you want to pull out for your Visnostic Statements are the client centric points. The most powerful things that all clients want to know are the **results.** Be sure and categorize all results. For example, reduction of costs, improve efficiencies, return on investment are typical declarations of results I have seen in almost every sales presentation.

After the content is separated into either vendor or client categories, I then create sub-categories under each main category. For example, I just recently evaluated a presentation and created the following breakdowns:

<u>Sample client-centric subcategories</u> –
Client challenges, complexity, results, outcome, miscellaneous content

<u>Sample vendor-centric subcategories</u> –
Vendor specific details such as jargon, acronyms, technical terminology, definitions, features and functions, and any other specific services or product details

The best way to properly learn the process is to have an actual presentation slide deck to dissect. Although I have access to many of the presentations of various employers, to avoid legal issues or any embarrassment to any of them, I will select a random slide deck to walk you through. I went to a website in which you may be familiar – https://www.slideshare.net. I did a simple search for "sales presentation" and flipped through several results from my query.

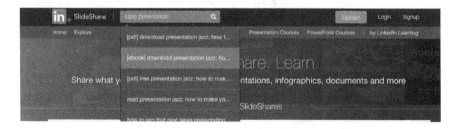

As I was sifting through the slide decks, the first thing I did was to look for a fortune 50 company to analyze. Then I went to see how many slides were in each deck. They ranged from 34 (the smallest deck I opened) to over 100 slides.

One of the cool things that I like about this site is that it will tell you on each slide the number of people that have "clipped" your slide. This often gives hints about which slides resonate the most. The problem is that you don't know with whom it is resonating. Is it someone stealing your data for their own decks, a client, a student, a competitor, or a coworker?

A clip notification also demonstrates which ones are NOT resonating as well. As you analyze your own deck, you may want to consider sharing it on a site like this. Not only will you be able to determine which slides are your most intriguing, but it also informs you of the number of times the deck has been viewed, comments, thumbs up, and number of times it was downloaded.

If you are exploring other company's decks, you can determine how old the deck is by how long ago it was uploaded. You can also share this by sending it to someone or even to yourself for future reference. You can also see how many views each deck has received.

Think about this for a second...if you have an awful marketing message that is vendor-centric, look at how many people know about it. In this case, it's being written about in this book AND as of February, 2019, it has been viewed almost 300,000 times. NOW imagine you have a GREAT marketing message that is CLIENT-CENTRIC...I wonder how many views THAT would get! I suspect MANY MORE! And who knows? I bet some viewers are potential clients. If the message resonates with the right audience, you may end up with some new clients with less effort than normal! So be sure and include your contact information on those slides!

Once you translate your current messaging and load it on this site, it's almost as impactful as your own website! It's certainly an additional channel that has potential to increase your client base!

As I flipped through multiple decks, I noticed that most of the statements in the decks are so generic in nature that it is difficult to determine what is being sold. These decks could be recycled and could be used to sell anything from software to home appliances. Does this sound familiar? It is exactly the same observation I made after my client fell asleep during my presentation and then zoned out a second time while doing his grocery list. So these problems still exist today; sounds like another proof point of my "Roast Story Syndrome."

Almost all of these presentations articulate that what they are selling will save money. They claim they are more efficient than the competitors or the incumbent provider. They brag about the ease of use while describing why their offering is better than the competitors. They basically describe how their offering will catapult their clients into Nirvana. But per our knowledge of Neuroscience, this approach misses the mark because these decks rarely answer WHY, HOW, or WHAT and more importantly, most decks do not nurture a dialogue or two-way communication. And the slides that do have visual aids often use charts and graphs. And while they can tell a pretty impressive story, some are so complex, that they often make the brain work way too hard. This makes it almost impossible to translate the meaning or decipher the story the client is looking for.

The reality is that most decks are created by individuals that are well trained to know what the current "in" colors are, the coolest fonts to use, what graphics can be used legally, the card stock on which to print them, and other cosmetically appealing details (marketing) OR they are created by those that understand HOW the product works (techies). **But very rarely have these deck creators ever purchased what they are trying to help the sales organization sell. See the** problem?

I apologize to anybody that currently has ruffled feathers but please bear with me. I want this knowledge to make its way into marketing departments all over the world, so I am writing this with the hopes that clients, salespeople, leaders, and marketing people all benefit from these words. **I am not saying that your baby is ugly. I am saying that I want to help you make your baby more beautiful, interesting, and effective.**

How many readers will admit that the first thing you do when you are about to get a presentation, is look in the bottom left hand corner of the screen to see how many slides you will have to endure?

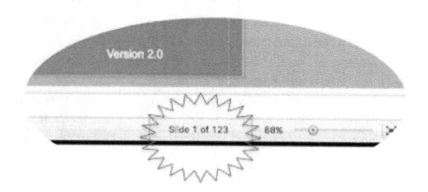

Yikes! **123 slides?** Flight instinct engaged!

Do you recall when you were in school and you walked into class and saw a projector or television, you were excited because you knew you were about to see a film versus enduring a lecture? Humans want visuals. We want to be entertained. We love stories. Presentations used to be super cool when the technology was new. Today, it is torture, not because presentations are outdated but because too many people don't know how to create them the way our brains want them to be delivered.

I am about to show you how to ditch the words to make your message less painful AND be remembered AND get your audience emotionally engaged! I am also going to show you a way to give this presentation without Internet, over lunch, on a golf course, or any other place that won't be technology friendly.

After sifting through dozens of decks, I found a presentation with thirty-two slides from a Fortune Ten company. They spent the first 12 slides explaining to the clients why doing it their current way was wrong. They also used those slides to brag about their own company's competencies and awards. How many readers have this same formatted deck? *The Challenger Sale* teaches that most clients don't invite salespeople back for the second meeting because we didn't tell them anything they didn't already know. In other words, we didn't provide value during the first meeting!

It wasn't until slide 13 that the deck started articulating what the client wanted to hear, which described the unique benefits of doing business with this Fortune Ten company. However, if the attention span really is only eight minutes, the audience has already disengaged. As I read through their points, I wondered if they even asked their audience WHAT was important to THEM before they made assumptions. By slide 15, the deck started getting into some technical features and functions.

While I was analyzing this online deck It wasn't until slide 18 that they started getting into the generic ways their software made life better. Why waste time with 17 slides the client wasn't there to learn? By slide 18 the client was already thinking about what they were going to have for dinner! My deck that my client slept through had this exact format! I know that if I were a buyer, I would do my research on a company before I invited them to my site to take up my valuable time. So do you really need those first slides talking about your company? Are they worth the risk of losing your audience's attention? **Ask yourself, if you only had eight minutes with your prospective client, which points would be the most important points to THEM? Find those slides and start your presentation with THAT information!**

Slides 19, 22, 25, and 28 were placeholders that were each titled "Demo" so the client actually got to see this offering in action. This made my analysis a bit challenged because there is nothing in the deck describing what they were going to be shown. The header in Slide 30 said, "Now, what are you waiting for?" I assume this was their attempt to flush out a sense of urgency in the client.

Overall, I would have given this deck a "D" grade and remember, it's been viewed almost 300,000 times! The final slide was a bio on the speaker. She appears to be a technology expert versus a sales professional or marketing expert. I wish there was a way to know what percentage of her presentations proceeded through the sales cycle. I suspect the number is very low. But in all fairness, I looked at other decks as well. I chose this one as an example because it is a Fortune 10 company and had the least number of slides.

All of the decks I reviewed seemed to follow the same pattern: build credibility, talk about industry pains, and then data dump all the specs about the offering. Most decks could really be done with one to three slides if we were to keep in mind what the audience truly wants. What if I told you that you could be more impactful with ZERO slides? That is the direction in which we are heading. You will learn more about this next.

For Step One of your own analysis, you should have been able to eliminate most of the slides. Only keep the ones that articulate results or differentiators to the clients. Leave out anything pertaining to your company, the stock price, etc. Keep asking yourself, "WHY would a potential client care about this slide?" As you go through your deck, note all the points that reference results. You will use these to convert your slides into your Visnostic Statements later.

The rest of these steps are fairly easy to read through because they are much shorter and on point.

Step 2 – Gather Your Case Studies or References

Our minds want stories and what better stories than those from our most successful and happy clients? Case Studies are typically full of the results we are looking for, but very few clients have legal teams that will allow them to be actual references due to fears of lawsuits from competitors. Clients love to help you and can give you valuable perspective from their point of view. Plus, you may gather additional off the record comments that got cut by legal when the case studies and results were originally constructed. Be sure and keep names out of your Visnostic Statements. Instead, memorize the details because this process tends to be interactive. Your potential clients will enjoy these stories of success as you walk through each Visnostic Statement. Keep a look out for results and timelines.

Step 3 – Creating the Visnostic Statements

By now, you have narrowed down the content in your presentation to only the details that will challenge your client to do things differently and you now have case studies. And the client centric content should now stand out with your highlights or notes.

Because this is the most important step, I have devoted an entire chapter to converting your presentation data into

Visnostic Statements. Chapter Three will go into greater detail with how to create powerful Visnostic Statements.

A major point worth mentioning now is that if you struggle creating these statements, this is a huge red flag. You will need to figure out if the problem is the current marketing content, poor training, lack of client success stories, or weak sales skills. Those that know the results of their offering will find the creation of VDS to be easy and fun to do. Those that don't understand your offering will struggle. Workshops can help if this is difficult.

Step 4 – Have Your Visnostic Statements Verified Internally

I recommend before you approach a client with the Visnostic Statements you converted, that you verify the accuracy of each statement internally. Also, run these by your manager and/or someone in marketing to ensure you have interpreted and converted the presentation and case study content accurately. The last thing you want to happen is that you misrepresent your company's capabilities or results. Great sales professionals do not lie or misrepresent their offerings.

Step 5 – Format the Columns Into a Spreadsheet versus a Document

I have mentioned multiple times that this process has evolved and one of these improvements is the formatting in a spreadsheet versus a document. Spreadsheets allow formulas to be written that will aid in the translation process and generate the client deliverable. I recommend that you work with your IT department to create formulas to calculate the responses by the client. Because what was developed at previous companies is the property of those companies, I commissioned someone I respect to help me create detailed instructions for my readers. This will be described in great detail in a future chapter.

Step 6 – Name Your New Tool

I have called these discussion tools by different names based upon the specific business I was representing. They have been called a "Pre-call Survey" when I used them to prep for a big meeting. I have also called the discussion process a "Health Check" and a "Free Assessment." I have even customized the name at various shows, events, and conferences to reflect the event name. For our purpose, I will refer to the tool as a Visnostics Tool.

Step 7 – Prototype Your New Tool with Current Clients

My favorite way to work out the bugs and revise this is to take a client that I have a wonderful relationship with to lunch. I basically recreate the story I told you earlier by asking the client to do me a favor by going through this process. In fact, I highly recommend doing this with as many existing clients as possible.

This tool may seem like it is just for new clients, but you may be shocked how little your existing clients really know about your entire offering. **This tool is a great conversation guide that will help you upsell your existing clients while strengthening your relationship.**

As I walked through the most recent tool I created, I realized it was way too long. I needed to get it down to the top ten statements. It actually took about six trial runs to identify the top ten that created the most emotions and interest. Most of these were universally appealing but there were a few that excited some of my clients and not others.

So I actually ended up with a top 15, which was a huge reduction from 30 original statements. I ended up keeping all the statements but "hid" them in my spreadsheet in case I needed them in the future. I also hoped that I would find a client that would appreciate a deeper dive into their assessment so keeping all the statements hidden yet available is a great practice.

Step 8 – Decide on a venue for delivering your Visnostic Statements.

A venue can be a location and it can also be the way in which it is conducted; it could be a hard copy or an electronic version for a tablet.

Each response can be saved in a spreadsheet, a hard copy, or on an application in the cloud. I use Survey Monkey as a cloud venue for assessing potential DynaExec clients. I simply post the cloud providers URL on my own website:

https://www.surveymonkey.com/r/TR73SMS

After a potential client completes the statements, the responses are sent to a dedicated company email address.

Assess Your Current Sales Management

1. DynaExec Assessment Survey

Most Sales VPs fail within 12 months. Take this brief survey to find out how your company would benefit from DynaExec.

1. We have full confidence in the sales and marketing management teams that are driving results.
- o We would LIKE to say this today but we currently cannot do this.
- o We CAN SAY this today and we are satisfied.
- o We CAN SAY this today but it needs improvement.
- o This is not important, it's not applicable, or I don't know.

2. Our marketing team has done a brilliant job translating features and functions into language that our clients understand.
- o We would LIKE to say this today but we currently cannot do this.
- o We CAN SAY this today and we are satisfied.
- o We CAN SAY this today but it needs improvement.
- o This is not important, it's not applicable, or I don't know.

3. Sales and revenues are satisfactory or exceeding expectations.
- o We would LIKE to say this today but we currently cannot do this.
- o We CAN SAY this today and we are satisfied.
- o We CAN SAY this today but it needs improvement.
- o This is not important, it's not applicable, or I don't know.

4. The current management team has a successful track record driving results and revenues.
- o We would LIKE to say this today but we currently cannot do this.
- o We CAN SAY this today and we are satisfied.
- o We CAN SAY this today but it needs improvement.
- o This is not important, it's not applicable, or I don't know.

5. A thorough market research has been performed and our company service or product is being marketed effectively.

- o We would LIKE to say this today but we currently cannot do this.
- o We CAN SAY this today and we are satisfied.
- o We CAN SAY this today but it needs improvement.
- o This is not important, it's not applicable, or I don't know.

6. Our messaging incorporates neuroscience in all messaging. Therefore, our sales have increased using Visualization Diagnostic Statements.

- o We would LIKE to say this today but we currently cannot do this.
- o We CAN SAY this today and we are satisfied.
- o We CAN SAY this today but it needs improvement.
- o This is not important, it's not applicable, or I don't know.

7. The current management team is 100% honest during the business reviews and is at least 75% accurate with forecasting sales.

- o We would LIKE to say this today but we currently cannot do this.
- o We CAN SAY this today and we are satisfied.
- o We CAN SAY this today but it needs improvement.
- o This is not important, it's not applicable, or I don't know.

8. The proper Lead Generation efforts are being made. The pipeline is healthy and growing with solid business leads and opportunities.

- o We would LIKE to say this today but we currently cannot do this.
- o We CAN SAY this today and we are satisfied.
- o We CAN SAY this today but it needs improvement.
- o This is not important, it's not applicable, or I don't know.

9. Our current clients are very happy and eager to be references. We leverage their success to build our business.

- o We would LIKE to say this today but we currently cannot do this.
- o We CAN SAY this today and we are satisfied.
- o We CAN SAY this today but it needs improvement.
- o This is not important, it's not applicable, or I don't know.

*10. Find out your results!

Provide your contact information such as your name, title, company, email address, and phone number and we will respond promptly with a FREE Assessment and recommendation!

Thank you for taking the FREE Sales and Leadership Assessment Survey sponsored by DynaExec! www.dynaexec.com

Step 9 – Arrange a Workshop and Consulting.

This step is optional but will catapult your success and expedite the development of multiple Visnostic deliverables. Workshops will get the right messaging in the hands of salespeople in just ONE DAY. However, my objective is to describe how to do this with so much detail, that you can do this without a workshop.

The first workshop was conducted before this book was even published and it was a huge success. Thankfully, the client agreed to allow me to share the format that was created during the workshop. It includes the 1-5 scoring system that was developed several years ago. It also includes the very important Segments (See Step One of creating VDS) column to help identify and organize the Visnostic Statements by vendor business or product areas.

Some examples of potential segment names include financial impact, hardware, software, consulting, and specific products and services. This Segment column is very important because it will enable users to quickly identify and organize the strengths, weaknesses, and moderate areas of your clients' current abilities.

Furthermore, segments will aid in pinpointing the areas to prioritize sales efforts. Segments can also reverse our translation back to which products or services sales will focus future efforts.

You now have finished learning about how to start gathering and evaluating the data needed to create the Visnostic Statements for your new Visnostics Tool. But as I mentioned previously, having people respond to your Visnostic Statement is basically just gathering data. **We must convert that data into valuable information.**

The next few chapters will dive deeper into creating your statements, I will then help you understand the importance of graphics, and I will explain how to convert that data into an impressive visual that your client will value and be proud to circulate internally on your behalf.

CHAPTER FIVE
CREATING IMPACTFUL VISNOSTIC STATEMENTS

From a Visnostic perspective, these three graphics are a fantastic representation to help you learn and retain the formula for writing outstanding Visnostic Statements. Can you guess the meaning?

Here is a hint –

RTH is the formula for creating the BEST Visnostic Statements!

I'm actually using an acronym here to prove a point. Do you realize how overused acronyms are today? From a Visnostic perspective, it is one of the biggest mistakes made today in Corporate America's sales and marketing departments. The chances are high that you will not remember the letters or what order they are in and your clients won't either. But the chances are very good that you WILL remember the graphics!

I'm messing with you right now because it's another of my little simulations and at this point in the book, your brain must be on overload. I'm just trying to wake you up a bit. **Hopefully by now, you have learned that one of the most powerful messages Visnostics evangelizes is that we must avoid making our clients TRANSLATE our message.** And RTH is just a reminder that acronyms force the client to translate what they stand for so we must stop that madness!

I was having a conversation with a reader and she kept using the acronym MSA. Coming from the software world, MSA stood for Master Service Agreement so I was having a really difficult time following the points she was making. It wasn't until well into the conversation that I asked what MSA meant in her world and it meant Marketing Specialist Agencies. Well that bit of info sure changed my understanding of our conversation!

As you learned from the Introduction, Simon Sinek's book, *Start With Why* points out that most marketing messaging starts out with the "What" and "How" companies do things. Instead, messaging should start out with WHY because that is the real reason clients buy.

Earlier, I went into detail how Visnostics compliment Simon Sinek's book, *Start With Why* because Visnostics is not "theory" – it's instruction for detailed EXECUTION of his theory. You should recall that Visnostics starts with **WHY/RESULTS** and then **HOW/TIMELINES**.

I do want to make a <u>very strong point</u> that not all Visnostic Statements are going to have Results and Timelines but the ones that have these components will often end up being your very best ones.

The best way for you to prove this point to yourself is to try some of them with your clients. Write as many as you can and invite your best client to lunch. Ask him or her to respond but to also let you know which ones resonated and triggered the most emotion. Mix in some Visnostics that have results and timelines with the statements that omitted them. Their reactions to them will validate this claim.

This is important because we are all taught in sales and marketing training, that people buy based upon emotions. However, if it were that easy, we could just end the book after the chapter ended. The problem with visualization is that we all have our own unique backgrounds so our visualizations are based upon individualized and unique backgrounds and history.

Remember that a Visnostic Statement is not a promise or claim that you can do something. It is a way to help uncover what is important to your client.

RTH =

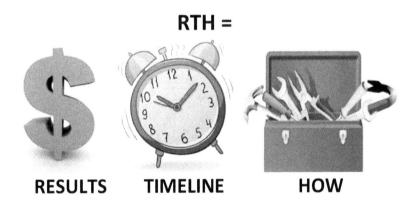

RESULTS   TIMELINE   HOW

Your messaging, communication, presentations, websites, and advertisements MUST have visuals and these visuals must tie back to your message...but only if you want your audience to

Relate (understand), Retain (remember), and Repeat (sell for you internally and give you referrals)

How to Convert Bullets to EFFECTIVE "Visnostic Statements"
There are two components to converting marketing messages into a Visnostic Statement approach. You will need the actual Visnostic Statements and then you will need to create appropriate responses. I know I am repeating myself but repetition equates to retention so always do your responses in threes so they are multiple choice and never allow the responses to be close-ended with a yes or no response. Close-ended questions will not engage the emotions you need from your participant.

Ensure the statements are positive.

Before I got married, I got some incredible advice from a counselor about raising children. The counselor described a scenario to me that took place in a packed grocery store and my future child was throwing a fit and embarrassing me. The scenario went on that my first instinct in that moment will be to tell the child that if he or she behaved, we could go get a new toy or get some ice cream after we are done grocery shopping. The counselor continued by saying that this tactic will probably work – in the short term. He said that if I take this approach in teaching my child, I would be reinforcing bad behavior by rewarding them for acting out. In other words, I just taught my child that if he or she misbehaves or embarrasses me, they would be rewarded. The counselor then told me that this same rule applies to my marriage and to my working relationships with managers, clients, and coworkers. Never back down, ignore, or concede to someone that is behaving in a manner that is unacceptable because you are reinforcing bad behavior. So what does this have to do with creating effective Visnostic Statements? Here are two examples of statements that say the same thing. Can you **FEEL** the difference?

- **Our sales numbers have increased 10% each quarter so I no longer dread Quarterly Reviews.**

- **Our sales numbers have increased 10% each quarter so I really enjoy Quarterly Reviews.**

Engaging the brain in positive visualization is a powerful approach. You read all the time about positive thinking and the power of positive thoughts. Therefore, it is imperative that when creating Visnostic Statements, that you are guiding the thought process towards positive energy, visions, and thoughts.

Despite doing these statements for over a decade, I just recently became aware of how important this advice really is. In fact, this past year I created a slide with a header that said something like, *Challenges Typical Clients Experienced BEFORE Becoming Clients.* There was a list of about a dozen scenarios describing how horrible things used to be. As this list was socialized internally, the content was not well received. By changing these "before" scenarios into "after" scenarios and rephrasing them into the client-centric language of Visnostic Statements, the responses became much more enthusiastic, not just internally, but with potential clients as well. People truly want you to paint positive visualizations versus negative thoughts and images.

Include Results when possible.

Because I hire salespeople, I have read hundreds of resumés. Surprisingly, most sales resumés are terrible. They ramble on about their territory, quotas, education, skills, etc. A hiring manager is very much a "Buyer;" and as a hiring manager, I want to read about results. Ok, so you had TOLA (Texas, Oklahoma, Louisiana, and Arkansas). I want to know how much you increased the pipeline and how fast you did it. While I like to know your quota, I really want to know how much you exceeded your quota. I am happy you had sales training, but how did you apply what you learned to become more successful? I would say that less than 10% of the resumés I've reviewed compelled me to want a discussion. Selling is exactly like interviewing. The client wants you to cut to the chase. What can you do and how fast can you do it to help them exceed their numbers?

Be careful that they are statements and not questions.

Do you recall when Strategic Selling and Consultative Selling were the desired approaches? I sold during those days and for the record, I am a huge believer in both the strategic and consultative sales THOUGHT PROCESSES. However, the approach around execution was extremely painful for the client and I avoid it at all costs. Often, it felt like some sort of competitive scenario with the client.

During my attempts at questioning clients, I noticed that the flaw in the consultative approach was that we almost became drill sergeants with our inquisitions. People do not like to be talked AT.

Therefore it should be no surprise that they don't like to be in the hot seat with a barrage of questions either. Asking questions is an extremely cerebral activity and can trigger the wrong emotions by putting the client on the defense.

Furthermore, filling out a questionnaire can be exhausting for all concerned and almost feel like an arm wrestling scenario.

Thankfully, this can be fixed very simply. The process will be so much more pleasant, for all concerned, by converting those questions into Visnostic Statements and having a more emotional versus cerebral conversation with the client.

Here is an example. Which of these sentences sound more compelling?

Do you consider training to be a cost or investment?
(Question)
Or
Our current training program has made us an additional 28% profit each quarter and is no longer viewed as a cost center.
(Visnostic Statement)

The magic of these statements versus questions is the way in which the brain has to process the data in order to respond.

To trigger the positive chemical reactions, you must gather the data without blasting the client with questions. Remember, you are there to help them, not to make them miserable.

The statement must be written as though the client is saying it, not you or your company.

Here are two statements. Which do you think will resonate with the client better?

- My company can save you one million dollars each quarter. (Vendor-centric)

- I save one million dollars each quarter. (Client-centric)

Avoid sounding generic.

A client also doesn't want to hear "We reduce costs..." "We save you money..." They hear this from every single vendor that walks in their door. They need and want you to be different. Let's start working on how we will help you be different.

Here is a typical bullet that most companies have in their presentation:

We save you money.

You probably have a bullet in your presentation right now that has something like this on it. Guess what? Your competitors do, too. This is so generic that you could be talking about retail items, outsourcing, technology items, natural resources, etc. Be more specific. **Don't make your client think so much.**

Where are the results to back up this claim? I typically find these details in case studies or reference documents. Here is an actual Visnostic Statement I re-wrote a few years ago:

I have reduced my costs by 23% in just six months after implementing similar software.

This wording answered the following questions:
- How do you save money?
- How much money do you save?
- How fast do you save money?

Their response choices to these statements would be, "I can say this today." "I WISH I could say this today." Or "I don't know, it's not important, or not applicable."

A Visnostic Statement should contain facts, numbers, or statistics especially about quantities and timeframes.

A good source for these types of details can often be found in case studies. I have mentioned numerous times that our minds WANT stories. The best business stories of how your company has improved another client's business can be found in case studies.

To create a Visnostic Statement, start with a result first to make the strongest emotional impact. A result could be an amount, timeframe, or both. By putting the results upfront, you immediately make a powerful emotional connection.

Then include how you did it. Try and map your feature/function slides to your case studies and you will have the ingredients for a powerful Visnostic Statement! Often you will find that as you go through this process, the client will ask you questions or ask for more details. It is a wonderful way to start a discussion around other client successes so you better know your reference clients very well.

This method of communication where the client actually asks you for details is the best way to make the information resonate. If you just put a case study printout in a collateral package, it most likely won't be read; and, if it is read, there is the risk of distractions or lack of concentration by the client/reader. If they are asking you for details, they are engaged.

Let's do another one for practice. The more details in the Visnostic Statement, the more mentally engaged your client would need to be in order to give an accurate response. However, be careful not to make the statements overly complicated or your client will get frustrated, confused, and annoyed. Here is another common claim by pretty much all companies:

We will improve your processes
and make you more efficient.

144

This is Vendor-centric (We) and doesn't address what your client really wants to know. How much? How soon?

"Most content in a presentation speaks from your company's perspective (We) but a Visnostics Statement speaks from your CLIENT's perspective (I).

How do you do it?

Convert that generic statement into something like this:

80% of the clients of my current vendor, report a decrease in human error by at least 90% and were able to reduce headcount by 20% due to automation.

This Visnostics Statement is written as though the client said it. It describes results of automation, amounts, and timeframe. Again, their response choices would be, "I can say this today." "I WISH I could say this today." Or "I don't know, it's not important, or not applicable." And as mentioned earlier, not all client responses will be affirmations.

By now you should be seeing a tremendous improvement after converting words from your company's perspective to your client's perspective. They both make the same point but one is much more detailed and impactful. And more importantly, one is much more meaningful to the person that matters most – your prospective client!

The WAY it is stated, requiring a response, is significantly more engaging. Statements, when worded positively, force your clients' minds to envision themselves as a huge success using your products and/or services. **This is how you eliminate the translation process!**

In the past, when clients responded by telling me that they could do or say it today, I considered this response to mean that I didn't have an opportunity to sell them anything.

Today, if the client states "I can say this today," ask them to grade themselves 1-5, with 1 being "needs a lot of work" and 5 being "it can't get any better." When I originally made this revision several years ago, it was due to a suggestion from my CEO. I was shocked how many grades were 3 or less which meant that clients were open to a better way.

This new grading system really opened my eyes to how many current areas in which clients want to do better. So there really IS an opportunity for improvement here and it is an excellent way to get the client to give you even more details about any struggles or dissatisfactions they currently have. I highly recommend using this grading system right away and don't be bashful about asking them to elaborate on why they gave themselves a particular score. I have been shocked how much I learn with this simple follow-up question.

Just because clients say they can do it today, doesn't mean they can't do it much better with your help!

I completely understand that this approach is not natural and can be difficult at first. If you need help, please send me your presentation and I will help you. Please use one of the emails I referenced. Once you get the hang of this methodology, the most difficult part will be to narrow down the Visnostic Statements to the best ten or less to make this process bearable for your client. I admit that this is my biggest weakness. I want to go through ALL the benefits because this becomes an incredible diagnostics tool to flush out all the ways in which I can help each potential client!

What a great problem to have!

_____

EXERCISE #4 –
Converting Features and Functions to Visnostic Statements

Here is an example conversion/translation exercise. Leverage the details from the Case Study to convert the original presentation bullets into Visnostic Statements. The responses from your client to your newly created Visnostics Statements should be "I WISH I could say this today! " "I CAN say this today." Or "I don't know, not important, or not applicable."

Case Study Details –
- XYZ Company became a client two years ago.
- They spent $1,000,000 in software & implementation.
- The software took six months to implement.
- They experienced zero down time during the conversion from the old system to the new one.
- The new system was more automated and reduced a fully loaded (salary, benefits, taxes) headcount valued at $150,000 immediately after implementation.
- Customer Satisfaction increased by 28% due to automation's elimination of human error.
- The new client won two new customers worth over $12,000,000 due to automation advantage over their competition.
- Client closed these new clients in less than 10 months.
- The return on Investment (ROI) was 12x the cost.

Original (VENDOR-CENTRIC) Presentation –
- We save money
- We provide a rapid ROI
- We increase revenues
- We improve customer service
- We help automate
- We reduce headcount
- We give our clients a competitive advantage in the marketplace
- We provide an easy and fast implementation
- We are better than the competition
- No business disruptions during implementation

Visnostic Statements (CUSTOMER-CENTRIC) –
Potential Answers in the Appendix

1. I saved _____ per year within ___ months of purchasing new software.
2. The ROI was ___ what I paid for the software in under _____ _____ of the purchase.
3. Revenues increased by _____ in under ___ years due to increased client demand.
4. Client satisfaction is at an all-time high thanks to _____.
5. ___ ___ ___ _ _____ _____ __ ___ _____ within _____ but more importantly; our new service is giving our clients a _____ _____ as well.
6. I am able to say we had an implementation that caused ___ _____.
7. I was promoted due to ___ _____ _____ _____ __ ___ _____.
8. Highlight all results and timelines in 1-7.
9. Which numbers had no Results or Timelines?

While sample answers are located in the Appendix, this doesn't mean that what you wrote was wrong. There really aren't right or wrong Visnostic Statements (unless they are inaccurate or ineffective). There ARE weaker or stronger statements. There ARE more impactful and more detailed statements. Some are impactful when they are simple. For example, I recently wrote one that stated "We have never been fined due to an employee being onsite and unqualified." This statement didn't have a timeframe or an amount but it definitely resonated. I was stunned how emotional the responses were to that one. It seemed that everybody said with passion that they WISHED they could say that today!

Practice them with your best clients. You will get better at this and you may be shocked how many things your existing clients either didn't know or they forgot. Don't be surprised if your first sales are from your existing clients! And you can close these sales during lunch or on a golf course! In addition to some easy and fast quota attainment, you will almost always get additional case study stories to incorporate into the next version of your Visnostic Statements.

Do you see the power behind changing a bullet that says "We save money" to "I saved $150k per year within six months of purchasing a new software." The second one answers how much was saved within what timeframe and how it was done. The details make it more impactful but having your client envision himself or herself saying it, is what triggers the brain to engage emotionally. This is exciting when you actually watch it work. This is what is meant by **"Sales and Marketing MUST do the translating for our clients!"**

When you declare that you can save money, it has the same exact impact on your audience as the binary code exercise. It's simply too much work and before you know it, they will be zoning out, thinking about personal things, or anything else to escape the boredom you have created for them.

So to summarize what we learned in Chapter Five, you should now understand how to create powerful Visnostic Statements by combining results from case studies with your current marketing message. You can now start converting generic feature/function or speed and feed statements into powerful Visnostic Statements by combining the results with the function details.

CHAPTER SIX
THE THREE R'S OF VISNOSTIC STATEMENTS
RETAIN, RELATE, REPEAT

Chapter Six will help you gather your thoughts on the type of visuals you will want to include in your final deliverable to the client.

Does your message tell a story that helps ensure your client can Relate, Retain, and Repeat?

The Three R's of
Visualization Diagnostic Statements™
Relate - Retain – Repeat

With the "Three R's" in mind, let's stop for a moment and reflect on the first story in this book. Remember the roast story with the mother and daughter? As you read this, what did you visualize? Do you see the drawings or do you see the letters in the story? Can you repeat the story?

What about the Christmas Story? Do you "see" the wreath? Do you remember the story? Can you tell it without the book?

What about the graphic with the little guy that had on boxing gloves and then another graphic of him running? What did that graphic represent? Can you explain it to others?

You could **RELATE** to those stories, which helps you to **RETAIN** those stories, so you can **REPEAT** them! Neuroscience is so predictable and so universally effective. Why aren't we leveraging more graphics that tell stories in our communications with EVERYBODY?

Don't we want our audience to relate, retain, and repeat our presentations to others within their organization? YES! So I ask you again, "Why do our marketing materials, slides, brochures, websites, and infographics have so many words full of features and functions instead of telling stories?"

Why do we prefer to watch videos on YouTube instead of reading the directions or instruction on how to do something?

What makes Instagram so much more appealing than other social media outlets?

The answer is that we want that visual translation done for us. We don't want our brains to do that work. We are only human. And guess what? The last time I checked, our clients are human too.

Ideally, marketing will create Visnostic messaging. However, if they don't, it is up to the salesperson to convert and translate those features and functions into something that the client can relate to, comprehend, understand, and VISUALIZE.

But here is the problem with that scenario; when a salesperson is forced to do this, they aren't selling. Relying on sales to do this is a costly decision but it's the only way I've been able to convert features and functions into meaningful Visnostic content that my clients are craving. I take full accountability for this disconnect because I've never been able to adequately articulate to marketing why this was needed. In fact, my most recent struggle is what inspired me to finally document my thoughts for future leadership roles.

This disconnect hasn't been marketing's fault; Visnostics aren't taught in college (YET) and most marketing teams won't learn Visnostics in a traditional marketing role. For marketing departments to stop the madness that is product marketing, they will have to change the way in which they operate and **THINK.** But why would they WANT to change if they don't understand what makes marketing messaging ineffective?

When was the last time your marketing team interacted with your existing client base? How does marketing create case studies or track ROI (Return on Investments) with clients? As marketing departments become more interactive with clients, they may uncover unique ways clients benefit that are excluded in the current messaging. Almost every story I've shared are examples of how marketing messaging has missed the mark with the clients.

For this to take place, marketing's role must evolve into a more client-facing position. In fact, I'd love to see marketing's participation in sales presentations to become the norm! And marketing should ALWAYS be included in any shows or conferences or booths. The ideal scenario would be for marketing AND sales to do those events together because each team brings their own special insight and experience to ensure clients get what they need and leave with a memorable and positive impression of the company.

Clients must understand the benefits of doing business with you, but **they must also be able to remember your value proposition and articulate it internally.** A great way for salespeople to gauge how they are doing is to look for signs that your clients **remember (RETAIN)** your main points, **comprehend (RELATE) to them,** and **become competent to share (REPEAT) your message internally when you are not available.** Having impactful visualizations are key to ensuring your client can spread your message and become a very effective Champion for you and your company.

VISUALIZATION AIDS MEMORY

Visnostic Statements engage the emotions and thoughts of your clients. You now know how to take existing marketing messaging and case studies to create powerful Visnostics Statements.

You will then review the statements with your clients and begin to collect their self-evaluation responses.

However, there is very little value in handing your client a document with your statements and their responses. This is just data and you aren't telling them anything they don't already know.

So now that you have the information that you need from the client, we can start to build your client deliverable. The deliverable that you give to the client must **paint a vision of what "COULD be"** versus giving your client a document full of what they just told you and they already know. So let's talk about why visuals will be an important element of the deliverable.

Basically, we have two ways in which to help others visualize our message. We can either paint a picture through our words and actions or we can literally paint a picture using graphics, photos, charts, or other forms of artwork. As sales professionals, we need to be able to do both.

Once you finish **translating** words from your brochures and presentations and **converting** them into Visnostic Statements, you are ready to create your deliverable. You have created a tool to gather data and diagnose your client's areas of weakness and strengths. However, data becomes valuable when it is converted into information. The final result will be a **memorable** deliverable for your client.

The Three R's – RETAIN
To Keep In One's Memory

The words retain and remember are interchangeable. I have found the best way to retain information is through visualizations and having impressive results in the content. So the first of the three R's actually includes the words retain, remember, and results.

Remembering names has always been one of my biggest challenges in business. So when I was in my 20's, I took a continuing education course to help me with memorization.
This class taught me to create "folders" in my brain for each person's name. So if someone told me that her name was Kristin, I should visualize a folder full of all the other Kristins I knew. The approach helped but I still stink at remembering names. I tried looking at names on badges but I can't recall names that way either. But I didn't give up on improving my memory.

I took another course a few weeks later that promised to help students remember the content of their presentations without index cards or notes. The syllabus even promised that students would learn how to make a grocery list without ever writing it down again.

This time, they taught us to envision our grocery items on parts of our body. We started at our feet. We were taught to imagine a carton of eggs on our feet, bananas stuck to our ankles, and a milk carton on our knee. You get the idea. I still do this today. And while it isn't perfect, it works pretty well.

As far as how to remember your presentation without note cards, the training advised going to the venue early and start at the left side of the room and envision your topics on the doors, windows, clocks, and other landmarks in the room. This also works fairly well. The audience thinks you are doing a great job scanning the people in the room and making eye contact with every person but you are actually focused on the items in the room like outlets, clocks, wall hangings, or furniture. Again, it works great but it's not always perfect.

Why am I telling you these stories? Because it is 30 years later **and I still remember both of those presentations, the RESULTS from the education, and I retained the methodology I was taught.** Neither of the classes used presentations loaded with words. The only slides they showed us were pictures of what they instructed us to do. The speaker stood in front of us and demonstrated how it worked and explained it to us and then the instructor had us work in small groups to actually practice doing it. Then each of us presented our unique grocery lists that we were given. They made us engage in the learning process and taught us what to do using PICTURES, not words. Despite feeling the need to take a memory course, I actually remember most of the details from that session all these years later! **The main take-a-way for me was that the visualizations from that training made me RETAIN details long term!**

Using effective VISUALS that actually relate to the messaging and ENGAGE the audience through execution is the key to memorable presentations!

Wouldn't you like each of your clients or potential clients to remember what you taught them? The secret is in getting them to visualize and engage. This should sound familiar. This is why your participation in the exercises is so important!

Remember earlier I suggested that a slide deck could be created without words? This chapter will help you take the results from your Visnostics Discussion and create custom presentations using very few words but using many visualizations and stories.

Think about what you learned in *What Great Salespeople Do.* You want to be telling a story with every point you make. The better visualization you create for your audience, the more likely you will be able to increase your chances of them remembering and getting engaged.

Telling a story AT them is not as powerful as INSPIRING THEM TO TELL THEIR OWN STORY!

As Dale Carnegie taught us almost one hundred years ago, nothing sounds sweeter than the sound of your own name. **Get the client to tell their story, and give that story back to them in a beautiful visualization and you WILL make an incredible impact.**

You must transform their responses into a deliverable that will have meaning and allow you to explain why you will be able to help transform their weak and moderate performance into additional strengths.

The Three R's – RELATE
Make or Show a Connection Between Making Visuals Personal During Meetings

Almost every sales book emphasizes the importance of establishing rapport with your client. In fact, there are probably more books written about Relationship Selling than any other topic. If it were easy, there would be no need for this type of training or education. **The words relate, relationship, and rapport are also interchangeable**. Using a

Neuroscience approach in the client/vendor communication process will help catapult relationships into a solid and credible status.

In the 90's I hosted a meeting in Colorado with executives from a Houston Oil Company. This was before Facebook and LinkedIn but we did have Google. So I searched for the attendees on their webpages; I searched for bios; and I searched for their names. It just so happened that the leader of the team popped up in my search because an article had been written about him and his miniature train collection that included an incredible photo of this man with his trains.

When the clients walked into the conference room to begin the meeting, this train photo of the senior level executive was projected on the screen with a "Welcome" message for the entire team. I also had a flip chart off to the side with every attendee's name hand written on the chart with space to the right of each name and a header above the blank space saying "Meeting Objective and Desired Outcome."

As each person walked into the conference room, the first thing they saw was a giant photo of their leader having fun with trains and a flip chart with each of their names written on it. You could feel the energy in the room as each attendee saw the photo as well as their own names. **This is extremely unusual for a sales presentation to start with the focus on the attendees versus the host company and its product or service being offered. Why?**

Most companies hosting clients will begin a presentation by projecting slides and photos of their own company. **In contrast, by starting a meeting projecting client centric information, the client will know immediately that this meeting was about THEM.** We did end up winning their business but more importantly the meeting kicked off with a fantastic icebreaker. Even the people working for him were unaware of this train hobby. We all learned a lot about the leader. He seemed more humanized and approachable and the rest of the meeting was very relaxed and even fun. By focusing on the client, what we also communicated was that our company culture was one in which they would want to do business. **A connection was established that made each person in that room RELATE to each other on an emotional level instantly.**

This was a powerful and positive impact on the overall feeling during the meeting thanks to the power of visualization. That meeting is remembered over ten years later by my coworkers and clients thanks to visualizations that were about them versus what we wanted to sell them.

If flip charts are not available, you can also use a whiteboard, add a slide to your deck, or create a sign-in sheet to pass around asking for contact information. Be sure you also include an area on the form to list each person's primary objective for a successful meeting. This will help remind the facilitator of the meeting to ensure that the audience members feel special by addressing and documenting each of their priorities in the meeting. When clients know you care about what they want to accomplish, they will return the courtesy by being more attentive. Acknowledging that their objectives are important is a powerful way to establish a strong rapport instantly.

The client input that is collected and documented will also help you with a recap email thanking the attendees and keeping track of any action items that were flushed out during the meeting. I will not dive any deeper into post sales meeting response and tracking because that will be the focus of Part Three in this series. A Joint Execution Plan will be created from what is gathered during the first meeting and will include actions, dates, and accountability details.

As you may recall reading, many salespeople leave meetings feeling that they nailed it. They witnessed the client heads bobbing up and down in agreement yet when they called for the follow-up discussion, the client went dark (ghosted them). Per the books on Neuroscience that I mentioned, this would be because the salesperson did not prove they provided adequate value in the first meeting.

If you research your clients prior to the meeting and ask them what they want to accomplish, the "Fight or Flight" instinct will be defused. This will aid in collection of the data that will be converted and translated into a valuable deliverable that will ensure that critical second meeting.

Imagine starting a discussion with a visual like THIS one:

How well do you think your client would RELATE to this approach? You will read a success story in Part Two using this approach during a meeting with a CEO.

The Three R's – REPEAT
Do Something Again or a Number of Times

Most salespeople don't consider that the audience they present to may not be the final decision makers. Even if you are selling to the CEO of a Corporation, often he or she must get approval by a Board of Trustees to protect stockholders and investors. Other organizations require a Steering Committee in order to make a decision. They must then be competent with your message so that they can present to other stakeholders for final approvals. This means that your message must be **REPEATABLE** without your assistance.

The Right Visuals with ensure all Three R's!

Once you have translated the data from the Visnostic Statements and categorized each segment by strengths, challenges, and moderate areas, you will design a customized deliverable. **This document should be simple enough that your client can take it and REPEAT your message with the same quality that you articulated.** Having the appropriate visualization in this deliverable is important. Be careful because many charts or graphs can be just as much work translating as a document full of words and letters. KEEP IT SIMPLE so the client can't fail as he or she shares the report internally on your behalf.

I personally don't like a lot of Gantt charts or bar graphs for visuals because they require almost as much thinking as the binary numbers translated in Exercise #2. I prefer dashboards like the one pictured here. I would change the wording on this to soften the bad news around weak performance. From left to right, I would label these Challenges, Moderate, Strengths, and Outstanding. I avoid words like Bad, Lacking, Weakness, or Average. These can trigger emotions that we don't want our clients to experience.

We want clients to know that we aren't judging or condemning them. We are here to help improve "non-strengths" into strengths.

You will convert the Visnostic Statement responses into a document you will return to the client. You may want to change the name of the deliverable but I call it *The Insight Report*. This report will summarize and compliment the client's strong areas. In addition, it will identify areas that are more challenging and need improvement along with an explanation of how you can convert the non-strength areas into strengths.

More importantly, this report will map your potential solutions to the client's weaker areas. This will allow you the opportunity to describe how you and your company will help those areas become strengths.

With visualization software companies like Tableau and Qlik, visual scorecards are becoming much more interesting to look at than those old fashioned bar graphs typically generated using a spreadsheet. Tableau awards thirty experts, the title of Zen Master each year. A Zen Master is working with me to help DynaExec clients maximize the impact of visualization in Visnostic Deliverables.

Here is an example of a visual that she created after reviewing the template that I had help developing. These can be customized during workshops or you can contract a consulting firm like Teknion Data Solutions to help create the right deliverable for you and your company.

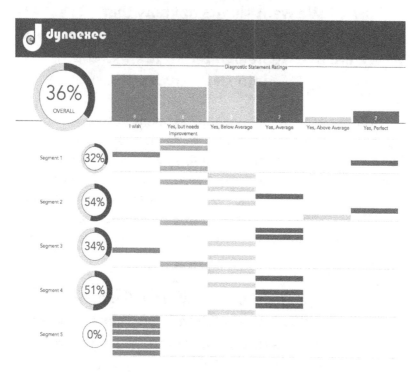

You may want to create additional value by including other comparative responses. Your clients will appreciate knowing how their performance compares to your existing clients, the competition, or perhaps other attendees during a conference. Other comparisons can be created based upon geography, segmentation, or an area specifically important in your industry.

Infographics have become extremely desirable the past five years. Having a format similar to this is visually appealing and easy to understand. Here is an example of a Pizza company (first column) and how they compared themselves to three of their competitors:

Creating simple visuals will help your client be effective as they REPEAT these results and their recommendations internally.

Your Visualization Visnostic Statements will be well received if they are accompanied by graphics that accomplish the **Three R's–Retain, Relate, & Repeat.**

DynaExec hosts Insight Workshops that will identify and develop a customized deliverable that your clients will value. This deliverable will practically ensure that you get that coveted second meeting and continue the sales process to closure. For more information, Workshop details are described in the back of this book.

Now that we have covered some ideas on visual aids, let's get into the most difficult content. Next, we will cover sample formulas to automate the Visnostics workbook that you have created.

CHAPTER SEVEN
Creating a Deliverable That Is Valued By The Client.

When you think of marketing tools, what comes to mind? Perhaps you imagine a presentation, brochure, website, an infographic, or a marketing video. I would agree that these are probably the most common marketing tools.

What if marketing gave sales an actual tool that helped translate features and functions into results that clients could visualize and understand?

What if this tool then translated the clients' visualizations into an insightful deliverable with graphics? What if these graphics told a positive story of the clients' strengths? What if this client story mapped your company's potential solutions to their non-strength areas? What if this mapping provided statement-of-work summaries that described how you could transform non-strength areas into strengths?

This deliverable is in a different league; it is something completely outside the box of what marketing typically creates. **Yet, it is something that clients will treasure and not want to discard or file away because they have helped create this amazing deliverable.** It will be different from what all the other stereotypical salespeople provide the client.

The salesperson will be viewed as a Client Business Strategist, not someone that will engage the fight or flight instinct. And they will have Marketing to thank for this incredible tool!

169

If you don't already have at least ten powerful Visnostics Statements written, you need to stop reading and go create them. After they are completed, be sure to identify a segment for each statement. These can include categories such as financial benefits, technology, consulting, additional services, training, legal, employee benefits, products, and any other offerings available from your company. I recommend you highlight each segment with a different color on your Visnostic Statement worksheet to make it easier to see the different segments/categories. This will help you sort and organize the statements into a logical flow. Start with your most compelling statements in order to make the quickest impact on your client.

This is the most important chapter and it may be the most difficult for many readers because it is technical in nature. Don't let that scare you. I encourage you to work with IT coworkers to create formulas specific to your tool. I worked with my favorite coding expert, Ryan Wicks, to create a workbook template that you might be able to leverage as a foundation for your own tool.

This chapter is also difficult to read because has very few visualizations. The biggest complaint I received from readers of *Visnostic Selling*, was that the screen shots were difficult to read. There was no way to make them more legible in a book with these dimensions so I removed them completely.

My goal is to eventually convert this spreadsheet into a software program or app. But for now, anybody can create a spreadsheet that will work. If you create a new tool, I would love for you to share your format!

For retention purposes, I have mentioned multiple times that our brains are a lot like a computer. Computers convert 1's and 0's to something on our computer screens that we can comprehend.

Character	Binary Code	Character	Binary Code	Character	Binary Code	Character	Binary Code	Character	Binary Code
A	01000001	Q	01010001	g	01100111	w	01110111	-	00101101
B	01000010	R	01010010	h	01101000	x	01111000	.	00101110
C	01000011	S	01010011	i	01101001	y	01111001	/	00101111
D	01000100	T	01010100	j	01101010	z	01111010	0	00110000
E	01000101	U	01010101	k	01101011	!	00100001	1	00110001
F	01000110	V	01010110	l	01101100	"	00100010	2	00110010
G	01000111	W	01010111	m	01101101	#	00100011	3	00110011
H	01001000	X	01011000	n	01101110	$	00100100	4	00110100
I	01001001	Y	01011001	o	01101111	%	00100101	5	00110101
J	01001010	Z	01011010	p	01110000	&	00100110	6	00110110
K	01001011	a	01100001	q	01110001	'	00100111	7	00110111
L	01001100	b	01100010	r	01110010	(	00101000	8	00111000
M	01001101	c	01100011	s	01110011	)	00101001	9	00111001
N	01001110	d	01100100	t	01110100	*	00101010	?	00111111
O	01001111	e	01100101	u	01110101	+	00101011	@	01000000
P	01010000	f	01100110	v	01110110	,	00101100	_	01011111

Our brains do the same thing when they convert letters and words to physical things that we visualize. This is a major point because I have observed that salespeople make their clients' brains work way too hard. The easier we make the analysis process for our clients, the more likely they are to see the value we provide and award us their business instead of our competitors.

Today, most salespeople give out the popular marketing tools and expect their clients to do the translating.

We also make our sales teams think too much. When done correctly, this tool can automatically map the potential solutions to the non-strength areas identified by the Visnostic Statements.

Once you have collected the responses your clients, giving them the Visnostic Statements with their responses means you would be basically handing them what they just told you. So you haven't told them anything they don't already know.

Where is the value in that? If you do this, chances are, you won't be invited back for the next meeting.

There was a story in *The Challenger Sale* that described a client's attitude towards a sales rep that they really liked. However, the client admitted that they purchased from her competitor because they were perceived as adding more value. Translating what your clients told you (Visnostic Statement Responses into something revealing (An Insight Report) is great way to add value.

With this approach, you WILL win business even if you didn't have a strong relationship at the beginning of the sales cycle. In fact, the credibility earned during this process will catapult your relationship status to an excellent rating! You will be on your way to becoming "an extension of your client's team" versus a "typical salesperson."

I hope you are starting to see how all the books I referenced earlier have started to complement each other. I know I shared a story about giving a filled out form to my client and he was thrilled with that as my deliverable, but that is rare and cannot be expected in every sales scenario. In addition, that was my first attempt at Visnostics and it has evolved and continues to evolve.

Let's discuss how you can create an incredible deliverable that your client will want to circulate internally. This deliverable is so powerful that it will transform your client into a coach, champion, and advocate. Why? They would love to create this for themselves but it's too much work so they will be grateful to you for taking that off his or her plate.

YOU ARE FINALLY
DOING THE WORK
FOR YOUR CLIENT!

So basically the Visnostic Statement process accomplishes the following milestones:

1. It allows the client to tell you how to sell to them.

2. It provides clarity in how you prioritize your sales discussions. I have sold software my entire career and most software is so robust (i.e. complex) that you would put your client into a coma covering all the areas in which your software will enrich their lives. So the Visnostic Statement exercise will uncover specific areas in which you can focus your sales efforts and spare the client (for now) from all the other alternatives you can provide.

3. You identify each strength and weakness. However, you are not calling them out or insulting them because (unlike typical presentations) the negative information came from them, not you. This is the power of engaging "metacognitive" within your clients. This point is the most powerful component of Visnostics and why I have it trademarked.

4. Even the areas in which they "CAN" do this today are scored. This scoring is one through five with one being that they do it today but it needs a lot of improvement and five being that things are perfect. So even a comment that says they can do it today can be just as

much of a sales opportunity as a response of "I WISH we could do this today."

5. Your client becomes emotionally engaged. The Visnostic Statement Methodology inspires them to envision scenes from his or her past or present. The "Money Exercise" proved the power in this approach; emotions will surface resulting in comprehension of your message much more effectively than a slide presentation.

But all of these points are just DATA. It is up to "The Challenger Sales Professional" to convert that data into valuable information and paint the vision of how the clients' lives will be improved.

Creating the Translation Formulas –

1. Create a workbook with four worksheets.

   Label the main worksheet Diagnostics. This is where your statements and client responses will reside. This is the only part of the workbook that your client may see.

   It is also the only worksheet that will be altered. All other sheets are static and should remain locked to avoid accidental modifications to the formulas.

   As stated multiple times, do not give this to your client electronically. Allowing them to see the formulas could take away the allure of your final deliverable. Notice the different shadings for each segment. This makes it easier to identify by offering.

This template is extremely scalable. When adding lines to different segments, just be sure you label the segments correctly and the formulas will pick up the addition and make the appropriate adjustments.

2. Create a worksheet called Formula Sources. This will be a reference used for formulas. This is also the location for the details of the dashboard. This is static and requires no alterations or edits.

	A	B	C	D
	320	= SUM(B13:B16) - SUM(B11,B19)		
1	0 - I WISH	0		
2	1 - Yes, but needs improvement	1		
3	2 - Yes, Below Average	2		
4	3 - Yes, Average	3		
5	4 - Yes, Above Average	4		
6	5 - Yes, Perfect	5		
7	N/A - Not Important, Unknown	N/A		
8				
9	Pointer Start Minimum	1		
10	Pointer Start Maximum	179		
11	Pointer Width (2 recommended)	1		
12				
13	Chart Series Green Width	60		
14	Chart Series Yellow Width	60		
15	Chart Series Red Width	60		
16	Chart Series Blank Width (Bottom)	180		
17				
18	Diagnostic Dynamic Chart Point Value	1.432		
19	Diagnostic Pointer Start Value	94.512		
20	Diagnostic Pointer End Value	264.488		
21				
22				
23				
24				
25				

FORMULA SOURCES / DIAGNOSTICS / DIAGNOSTICS CALCULATOR / DIAGNOSTICS CHART

3. Create a worksheet called Diagnostic Calculator. This area will calculate the totals for each of the Segments. For example, if a segment has two statements, the

possible high score would be 5x2=10. But if you have a segment with 10 statements, the possible high score would be 5x10=50. So a 10 on the first example would create a dashboard in the green (strength) area, while a 10 on the second example would create a dashboard in the red (challenges/weaknesses) area.

This is also the area that has formulas stored. Once you have the first line of formulas, the other lines can be slightly modified to complete your worksheet. Here are some examples of formulas:

B2 = COUNTIF(DIAGNOSTICS! $F$8:$F$107, $A2)

C2 = ($B2 - $F2) * MAX('FORMULA SOURCES'! $B$1:$B$7)

D2 = SUMIFS(DIAGNOSTICS! $B$8:$B$107, DIAGNOSTICS! $F$8:$F$107, $A2, DIAGNOSTICS! $C$8:$C$107, "", DIAGNOSTICS! $D$8:$D$107, "")

E2 = COUNTIFS(DIAGNOSTICS! $F$8:$F$107, $A2, DIAGNOSTICS! $C$8:$C$107, ">""")

F2 = COUNTIFS(DIAGNOSTICS! $F$8:$F$107, $A2, DIAGNOSTICS! $D$8:$D$107, ">""")

C2		fx	= ($B2 - $F2) * MAX('FORMULA SOURCES'!$B$1:$B$7)					
	A	B	Your Possible Score (Based on Applicable Challenges)	"I can do this today" Total Score	"I WISH" Items	"Not Applicable" Items	Industry Average	Our Average
1	Segment	Total Items						
2	Segment #1	8	35	19	0	1		
3	Segment #2	2	10	2	0	0		
4	Segment #3	14	60	26	2	2		
5	Segment #4	2	5	5	0	1		
6	Segment #5	4	15	10	1	1		
7								
8	All Segments	30	125	62	3	5	0	0
9								

This template has five different segments but this is not the limit. If you want to add more segments, you simply copy Row 6 and paste it in Row 7 and the formulas will modify automatically.

Columns G and H are not completed but are represented because it is intended to house data from collections to be averaged. Examples would be comparing individual responses to totals from an event or your client base. This will not be covered in this book but it is covered in the workshops.

4. Your fourth worksheet will be called Diagnostics Chart. This is where your graphs will be created automatically. You will save these charts for you final deliverable.

Once these four worksheets are setup, you will create a fifth worksheet that will be the deliverable. I like to call this a "Client Insight Report." You can change this name to match the objective of the deliverable. The workbook template calls it "CLIENT INSIGHT REPORT AND RECOMMENDATIONS FOR INCREASING STRENGTHS"

I designed this page so that when you fill out the Diagnostic sheet, it will populate these fields to avoid redundant entry. It looks a lot like the Diagnostics page. However, Column G has "Proposed Plan to Increase Strength." This is where you will explain how you will enable the prospective client to turn their challenged areas or moderate areas into strengths.

You may be tempted to simply put the name of the product or service in here but that is counterintuitive to everything you have just been taught! Never give them a product name. Work with your technical team such as Implementers or Consultants to summarize the PROCESS that will take place to improve the performance. If you put a product or service name, you have just gone back to your old ways of forcing the client to translate your terminology into what they can understand.

Most likely, you will need to reorganize these line items. Keep them in order by segment when filling out the statements but later, you will want to sort them based upon the scoring and level of strength identified.

Always start with the good news, which includes the strongest areas. This will be accomplished based upon the scores by segment. For example, if someone says "I can do this today" and they scored a 5 in each of five statements, their score would be 25 out of a potential 25. That would be a strength area.

Diagnostic Results

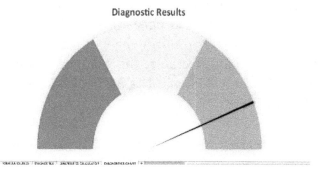

However, if they responded "I WISH" in those five areas, these areas will be identified as "non-strengths." The template I provide has predefined scores in the algorithms. However, these scores can be edited if you determine different scores would be more appropriate for your business.

Diagnostic Results

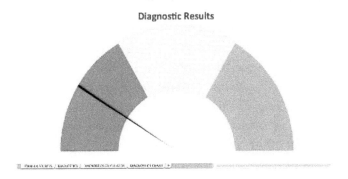

You will also have a midrange score that you also want to call out in your report as "Potential Improvements." With the two areas in which you identify as non-strength or as a potential improvement area, you will then have the opportunity to give a summary of how your company can turn these non-strength areas into strengths.

Diagnostic Results

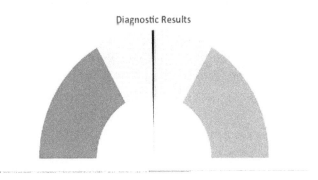

If you conduct a workshop with DynaExec, I will provide a spreadsheet template to get us started. Or your IT department can help you fill out the form automatically based upon the Diagnostics your client fills out.

You may want to enhance your Insight document with other charts and graphs offering comparative rankings. And the best way to do that is to track all responses you receive and let your client know how they compare to others. For example, if you were at a show or conference, your goal would be to conduct as many of these diagnostics as possible. You can then collect all responses and let each one know how they compared to other attendees at that specific event or show. These comparative visuals could also be based upon verticals or competitor responses.

With this insight report, you will have a fantastic reason to follow-up after the show with each person you interviewed. This should help you get that coveted face-to-face meeting after your event. **You would never want to just send the Insight report to your client without being there to walk him or her through it.**

Another great way to approach this is to first contact at least ten existing clients and go through this process with them. Collect all those responses and use your client responses as your baseline. You can then approach potential clients and compare their answers with your client answers. In theory, the non-clients should score well below your existing clients, which will demonstrate true improvements to the potential client. This is actually my favorite approach because if you created the right Visnostic Statements, your clients should respond with 5's on all the "We CAN say this today" areas. This sends a strong message to your **potential** clients that your **existing** clients are confirming the accuracy of your statement results. In addition, this should make your prospective clients eager to join in on the success!

There is one final bonus for taking time to interview your client base with Visnostic Statements; if you have a segment offering that your client was unaware, you may find yourself with an extremely easy revenue growth opportunity!

There are two areas in which your client will see the most value. The first will be comparing how they do things today with another category. But the most impactful information that your client wants and needs will be your response how you can convert their non-strength areas into additional strengths.

Finally, here is a word of caution as you design your deliverable; do not attempt to use their own words to "customize" your potential solution! You may be tempted to coincidentally map your products or services exactly to their needs, but you risk losing credibility, trust, and the relationship. Do not insult their intelligence by just repackaging what they told you as your deliverable.

Once again, I am looking forward to hearing from readers on creative modifications of these deliverables. Please send copies to me so I can recognize your efforts in future editions.

If all this still seems overwhelming, don't hesitate to reach out for assistance. **Visnostic Sales and Marketing is powerful but this tool is the real gold mine you should get from this book.**

Other Ways To Add Value with Visnostic Statements!
I participated in a rather large meeting with a client that had been in merger and acquisition mode. The audience was full of people from all over the country. Almost all of them were from locations that had been acquired and were now teammates and yet they were all meeting each other for the

first time – during my presentation! As we were planning for the meeting, we predicted that there might be some reluctance to share information with us because members of the audience may be uncomfortable with the newly formed organization.

Many people in your audience may be concerned about job security; therefore openly discussing their individual challenges didn't seem like the politically smart thing to share with a room full of strangers. So we leaned on the sponsor of the meeting. He shared with us important background on each team and several individuals. We went into that meeting knowing which people were the decision makers, what topics to avoid, what challenges had already been uncovered and we created a slide that was full of Visnostic Statements.

I know that this contradicts pretty much this entire book because the slide was full of bullets and letters. However, it ended up being the only slide we showed all day because the silence and reservation from the audience transformed into stimulating collaboration. The audience realized they each were experiencing many of the same challenges and had empathy for each other. This was an incredible scenario to witness. We were no longer salespeople. We became facilitators of a valuable conversation and team building exercise. We became Business Strategists versus that horrible stereotype associated with Salespeople. We even changed our titles after this meeting.

I wish there was a cookie cutter methodology that every single one of us could use on every single client. That would make things pretty easy. **However, the beauty of sales is that each client and each sales process is like a fingerprint; while they all look very similar, they will each be unique.** How you deliver your message will be dependent upon each unique client and diagnostics outcome. However, here are some tips that I believe will ensure your success:

1. While this approach is much more flexible than a presentation, it is important that you conduct the Visnostic Statements in person. Never hand the tool to the client and ask them to fill it out and return it to you. You will be missing out on the important body language, the collaboration, and the elaborate responses. You will learn more during the client's envision process than the responses themselves. In most conversations, I can't write fast enough because the client has so much they want to share.

2. Always reach out to the client **within twelve hours** of leaving your meeting with a summary of what you discussed and a timeline from which they can expect a deliverable If you wait longer than that, you and the conversation will be a distant memory and you will have lost your momentum and the client's interest.

3. Always set a date and time for that second meeting to go over the results in person. Again, do not be tempted to email the Insight report to the client. You will miss out on important dialogue and body language. Be face-to-face for that meeting to ensure you have 100% of their attention and they aren't asleep or creating some sort of to-do list.

4. Print out and keep hard copies of the Visnostic Statements with you at all times. These conversations can happen at any location, any time, and do not need

any technology to be conducted. Take advantage of that!

5. Also keep copies on your mobile devices. I like to send copies to my iPhone and then open and save it in my iBooks. You never know when that electronic copy will come in handy.

6. Work with marketing to design graphics that represent each Visnostic Statement. Showing graphics as you go over the statements will make a huge emotional impact that will be remembered.

I predicted this chapter would be more difficult to read. For one thing, cartoon drawings were replaced with screen shots. And most of the screen shots were actually too difficult to read so they were eliminated and not replaced. In addition, the first three chapters were written with more emotional content and hopefully you felt your own enthusiasm brewing as you read. However, due to the nature of the technical content, the last chapters were extremely cerebral. Remember that people buy based upon emotion, not logic. This is because humans enjoy feeling various emotions. While some people do enjoy cerebral content, the majority of people prefer to be entertained and have their feelings engaged.

While this chapter SHOULD generate the most questions, not one single reader has asked me for help which makes me suspect that readers stopped reading when they got to this chapter which is unfortunate.

If for some reason you still don't feel prepared to go execute these new skills, I offer three different types of one-day workshops to ensure success:

1. **Creating Visnostic Statements**. This is typically done with marketing and sales. We evaluate existing content and translate it by segmentation.

2. **Creating the potential solutions that map to each Visnostic Statement**. This is typically conducted with consultants, engineers, implementers, and technical support personnel.

3. **Sales Training.** In addition to the new tool, the content in this book should also inspire the creation of new presentations, brochures, infographics, videos, websites, and other corporate messaging. However, I see great things created all the time that fail because execution didn't happen at the field level. I will teach the concepts and stories of this book to the sales organization to ensure they are passionate and confident in the various ways these tools can be leveraged.

I look forward to working with as many of you as possible to ensure your success!

CONCLUSION

Congratulations for investing time to learn about Visualization Diagnostic Statements! I look forward to hearing from each of you about the ways in which it has touched your life and your clients' lives as well.

This book was written differently than most business books you have read in the past. I have been using specific tactics to help you retain the information you just read. Let's see if it worked; try and repeat what you read when you saw these graphics.

Did Fight or Flight pop into your head?

Do you remember the story that went with this next graphic?

What were the lessons learned during the exercise that leveraged this drawing?

Wouldn't you love it if your clients thought of the benefits you could bring to their organizations after seeing specific pictures? Wouldn't it be awesome if your clients could repeat your presentation internally? If so, you now know the secrets to making that happen!

The steps you just read are things that I have never documented and have only partially shared with various sales teams that reported to me.

I have guarded this approach because I believe one reason these Diagnosis Statements are so powerful, is because nobody else does them. I am concerned that if this approach takes off, it will lose its magic.

So if you are one of the first to read this, I hope you have a sense of urgency to get out there and execute before millions of other salespeople start doing the same thing and it loses what makes it unique.

I want to stress that this is not a hypothesis. This approach has made me exceed my sales numbers when not one other salesperson on the team was able to hit quota. It was my secret to being the number one salesperson globally three years in a row with a very well-known Japanese technology company. It feels good to share these secrets at this stage of my career and I am extremely excited to hear new stories of success from my readers. I fully expect to learn new and creative ways to execute this communication methodology from each of you.

I hope you were able to read this book in one sitting. My goal was to keep this book short and sweet because these concepts are new and can be difficult and time consuming to execute. But do not get discouraged if this feels uncomfortable. These feelings will subside because you WILL get better at this after you do it a few times.

I don't expect you to have passion for this approach after just reading a book. However, I DO expect that you will feel the same passion I have for this approach the first time you witness its power with your clients!

You have learned specific ways you can execute fundamentals from all three books mentioned in the Preface. My book focused on Why, How, and What needs to be done. Stories were in each chapter to help with memorization. In addition, graphics were a big part of this book to help with retention and to quickly reference specific areas. And finally, this is a very different sales approach and you have learned a unique way to challenge your clients to do things differently and better.

All three of these recommended books stated either blatantly or subliminally that the most successful salespeople add value and do things differently than their competitors. The Visnostic Statement approach is unusual and when done correctly will be welcomed by your client. This approach will defuse the Fight or Flight instinct. You will earn your clients respect because you will clearly paint a picture of how you will not only help them be better in several of their non-strength areas, but you just did most of the work for them in order to circulate your value internally. You will see your client become your biggest champion and coach because you just described how you could make them look good and catapult their career. You will now be a trusted advisor instead of a typical salesperson trying to earn a commission check.

You should feel differently about yourself. Because of this new knowledge, I challenge you to reflect on your current title. If it is a sales title, account manager title, or anything that implies sales **I highly recommend that you consider changing your title immediately!** Even Mike Bosworth suggested changing titles in his Foreword. Do you recall what you learned about the Fight or Flight instinct within each of us? Why in the world would you have a title that discourages people from meeting with you? As you use this approach, you will become much more than a salesperson so your title should reflect that. I love the title, "Client Business Strategist." What client wouldn't want to meet with someone that has a title that is focused on THEM? And who doesn't appreciate someone that has a position that is intended to help clients with strategic execution?

Once you are confident with conversations leveraging Visnostic Statements, and especially when you start seeing the deliverables that you will be generating, you will no longer feel like a salesperson anyway. Better yet, your clients won't view you as a salesperson either.

Hold your head up high because you will become a true trusted advisor and once your clients start telling other clients about their experience with you, your career will soar. I am excited for each and every one of you but I am even more excited for your clients. They need this translation effort from you and they will appreciate you for doing the work for them.

Not only did you just read a book that can change the way you perform professionally, but with proper execution, it should also change your company and your clients' companies for the better! Please be sure and share your comments, suggestions, and stories! I look forward to reading every single email! I expect this book to go through multiple revisions based upon feedback I receive and stories shared with me, but I also look forward to providing the next two books very soon.

It was important that Part One of my series focused on sales success because this book will immediately increase sales revenues. Once I have the attention, credibility, and respect from sales leadership, then they will be more receptive to what I have to share about leadership practices that must change.

Now that you have read the entire book, how has your interpretation of this graphic changed the first time you saw it?

Lastly, as you read this explanation at the beginning of the book, it was probably a bit confusing. As you re-read it now, it should make more sense.

WHAT are Visualization Diagnostic Statements™?

NOTE - Also referred to as a VDS, Visnostic, or Diagnostic Statement in this book.

A Visnostic or Visualization Diagnostic Statement is a trademarked term created by Kimberlee Slavik, CEO of DynaExec. It is a statement that requires a response from an audience. It stimulates emotional responses inspiring your audience to maximize their interest in your message.

The statements typically **translate** features and functions into something more meaningful to the audience.

A Visnostic Statement often originates as an ineffective, generic, one-way **self-focused** message that has been converted into a meaningful two-way engaging statement that is **audience-focused**. Existing presentations, brochures, case studies, and other marketing materials are often reworded to become Visnostic Statements.

A Visnostic Statement is also a qualification tool that will help you assess your audience. As you go through the statements, if your participant isn't responding or is struggling with responding, chances are high that you aren't in front of the right participant.

A Visnostic Statement is also an effective way to determine if sales and marketing currently have the right messaging. If creating these statements feels effortless, the current messaging is strong. When these statements are difficult to create, the content doesn't contain what the clients need and want to know.

What's coming in Part Two –

Visnostic Selling basically consists of almost everything you read in "Part One" of *Visnostic Sales and Marketing*. My goal was that the next edition would include an addition called "Part Two" that would be full of reader success stories. What I wasn't expecting was how quickly these successes would fill a new book.

Part One was very focused on a specific and powerful sales execution methodology. Part Two will focus on areas in which readers, including myself, have grown and evolved by executing Visnostics taught in Part One.

I am confident that the second half of this book has many reader successes that you will find invaluable. I hope to include YOUR success stories in the next release!

PART TWO:

READER SUCCESSES

SUCCESS ONE
PRESENTATION IMPROVEMENT

*V*isnostic Selling was published February 1, 2019 and the first six months were a whirlwind as readers followed the instructions and reached out to me. Over 150 reader discussions later and I have grown just as much in my Visnostic skills as THEY have! I have learned so many new ways to use this approach and look forward to uncovering even MORE ways they can be used in the future!

This is one of my all-time favorite success stories that I can't wait to share with you:

Every reader that emailed me their results of the "Money Exercise" and the "Binary Code Exercise" were offered additional coaching that was intentionally left out of the book. I then offered to give each of them $1500.00 worth of FREE coaching.

One of the people that reached out, works for a great technology company that just went public. He explained that he knew that his presentation deck wasn't Visnostic but he wanted to be a good "Corporate Citizen" and present what marketing had created. He was hoping I could help him find the right words that would ensure he stayed true to the message the company mandated, while making it as impactful as possible with Visnostics.

He added that he was the SEVENTH salesperson to present to this company and nobody made it past that first meeting. He was extra nervous because the CEO was actually going to be in attendance.

I had him present to me while I recorded it. I planned to transcribe it to help him find the client-speak points to emphasize. However, once he was done presenting, there was no need to transcribe it because it was blatantly obvious to me what needed to be fixed.

I told him that his first seven slides were full of data points that the client will not care about. These slides included history of his company, details around the IPO, (Initial Public Offering), information about the Executives and the Board of Directors, the growth trends, competitive comparatives, and the technical evolution of his company's offering.

In fact, there was only one slide that even mentioned why clients cared, which was what???? That's right – RESULTS!

I asked what all he knew about the CEO that would be in attendance. I suggested he read last year's annual report because it's basically written by the CEO and is full of the strengths and weaknesses of the company's performance. It also summarizes and justifies the CEO's priorities and initiatives for the current year. There is no better formula, in my opinion, to develop your messaging; you will learn everything you need to map your offerings to the CEO's priorities.

I then helped him word these points using the RTH formula (Results, Timeline, and HOW you do it). We found the CEO's photo and put it smack in the middle of a slide. We then created statement bubbles full of the Visnostic Statements we translated from several feature/function bullets in his deck. The slide looked like the graphics you see on all my book covers. However, instead of faceless cartoon characters, we placed a photo of the CEO. Each statement was written in the

First-Person as though the CEO was saying each of them. To the left of the photos and bubbles is where we put the three choices – "I can say this today, I WISH I could say this today, or it's not important or applicable."

I told my reader that as unnatural as it feels, that he should start his presentation with this CEO slide and then "let nature take its course." He was exceptionally nervous because this presentation was the next day and he still had a lot of research work to do to perfect our draft Visnostic Statements.

I then told him to move the slide that had the content with client results to the second position and move all his company information to the last part of the deck. I told him that once he had the "diagNOSTICs" flushed out with the CEO slide, he will know the right words to say with all the other slides. But I also predicted that he won't even get to them.

The next day, I received a call from my reader and he was laughing and extremely excited. He was still in his client's parking lot when he called me to tell me my prediction was 100% accurate!

He told me that the CEO had an extreme physical reaction when that first slide with his photo went up. And my reader told me that he could actually FEEL the instant rapport that was established from that single slide! The CEO was smiling as he read his bubbles and then he basically talked for almost the entire meeting validating each of those bubbles as things he WISHED he could say today and WHY!

Have you ever received this type of reaction when you asked those qualifying questions you've been trained on so diligently? NO! Because questions don't engage the brain in this manner!

When there was only fifteen minutes left of the meeting, my reader politely interrupted, in the interest of time, to ask if the CEO would like to see any more of the presentation and he said no, that he saw enough to know he wanted to move forward with him and his company.

My Reader was thrilled because this was the first time any salesperson had made it past the first presentation! The CEO even locked down a date and time for that second meeting.

But the real validation was after the meeting, the CEO came up to him and told him that he was the best salesperson that he had ever seen and he actually thanked him for not starting out with slides about his company!!! His first slide sent a strong message that this presentation was about the CLIENT, not the VENDOR!

After putting his story down in writing, I followed up with him to see how things were going. This is an excerpt from this response:

Hey Kim! Visnostics is going great. I presented to 4 execs today, and my first slide was headshots and quotes. As we were chatting after our meeting, getting ready to head out, one asked me where I got the pic and said, "Nice touch. You caught my attention." I've been pointing friends/colleagues to your book...I keep having success with Visnostics.

I shared his story with another reader recently and she told me that she had the same exact experience and also received a very similar comment! Both readers were actually THANKED by their audience for NOT presenting about their company!

The reader told me that he was ordering several more books because he was going to send copies to his Sales VP and his own CEO and recommend I come in and work with marketing to get their messaging converted.

I'm still waiting on that call but the passion I've seen from my readers, after they see Visnostics work, has fueled me this past year. I am a salesperson, not a writer but seeing and hearing about these types of successes has motivated me to stay focused on getting these final books out so I can eventually get back to work; I'm ready to get out in the field and help create more reader success stories like the ones you are about to read!

Another story that I have to share is about a rating I received: This whole "author" world is such a scam. When someone buys one of my books, I have zero idea who bought it because the bookstores and distributors consider each reader to be THEIR client, not mine. So your privacy is protected by the source from which you bought my book! That means, I don't know anything about my readers unless they reach out to me!

I do keep a close tab on the reviews of my books but only one time have I seen a review from someone that I haven't had a discussion. This person gave *Visnostic Selling* a great review but he only gave it four stars instead of five. When someone writes a review, I actually DO get the opportunity to respond. So I wrote him a private message thanking him for the positive review and offering him a free coaching session. He accepted and we had a conference call that went very well. In fact, he told me that he wanted to setup a workshop with me so I could work with his entire sales team. As we were hanging up, I asked him what I could do better in order to get FIVE stars instead of just four and I really respected his answer!

He told me that he wished I had provided a better understanding how to leverage Visnostics through an entire sales process. He wanted to know how to use them to prospect, to get meetings, and to close deals.

What great feedback! I plan to send him a copy of this second edition so he will be able to go change my one-and-only four star rating to a five star rating! I take all recommendations very seriously so if there is something YOU think would make future editions better, please email your thoughts.

Visnostic Sales and Marketing is what it is today because of feedback from my first six months of readers! I wish I could thank each and every one of you personally. But as I said, I don't know you exist, unless you reach out to me! Hint Hint...

I am thrilled to share how people have leveraged the RTH Formula to get interviews by writing more compelling cover letters. Readers have been selected for better jobs because their resumes were more powerful, they have stopped selling based upon price by uncovering ways their products and services are far superior than their competitors, and clients have embraced Visnostic Readers during presentations because rapport was established from the first Visnostic Slide!

The biggest revelation is that Visnostics is so much more powerful than just a STATEMENT, it's a completely different way to THINK about constructing your communication content!

I've actually mentioned this point multiple times in various different ways during Part One. With the following reader examples, I hope the magnitude of this point becomes even more crystal clear.

I'm thrilled to share this very important Part Two in this latest edition because even though I still wrote the content, it's about THE READERS!

I hope these success stories inspire you to send me your own successes! Happy Visnostics to each of you!

SUCCESS TWO
RESUME AND COVER LETTER –
PUTTING RESULTS FIRST

One of my college buddies was feeling old like me one day. Despite being a sales superstar for the past thirty years, Corporate America appeared to want to put him out to pasture before he was ready. After sending out dozens of resumes with personalized cover letters, he simply wasn't getting invited to interview anymore. He was sure it was age related.

The first thing he did after reading the first two chapters of *Visnostic Selling*, was to rewrite his cover letter and the first company he sent it to, responded immediately and even commented that it was the best cover letter they had ever read! He has given me permission to share it but asked that I delete the details so this is just an excerpt of the part that included his Visnostics:

COVER LETTER LEVERAGING VISNOSTICS

My name is Jeff XXXXX. I follow XXXXXX on LinkedIn & Career Builder site. I recently saw a Territory Manager position in the South-Central area I am drawn to because of my past medical sales success and being a top 5 candidate in recent interviews (w/XXXX XXXXX) for the XXXXXX position in Austin, TX.

I also have a close friend (XXXX XXXXX) in the CEO of the XXXXX who has written me a recommendation letter included in this application.

I invite you to read the brief statements about your salespeople below:

Can you say yes to these statements? If yes, then rank 1-5, 1 being needs improvement, 5 being outstanding. Or, maybe these statements don't apply?

- Our salespeople have infectious energy and enthusiasm resulting in sales of $1.4 Million.
- Our sales increased 10% from just the strong inner drive from our salespeople.
- Our salespeople convey meaning to the bigger picture around them, and they give our clients a sense of comfort and stability in the face of uncertainty.
- Our salespeople quickly weigh alternative paths and determine the best one for our client's success.
- Our salespeople pick up and absorb information quickly and they challenge themselves to learn more to keep themselves on the cutting edge.
- Our salespeople have an exceptional ability to win others over.
- Our salespeople have a deep sense of dedication and feel ownership for their commitments.
- Our salespeople have a natural ability to coordinate people and resources for maximum effectiveness.
- Our salespeople core values guide them and give them purpose.
- Our salespeople trust their instincts, so they forge ahead confidently, even on risky paths.

If you answered mostly no or your points add up to less than 30, I will add immediate value to your salesforce. If your points added up to greater than 30, I will expand your value on a great team.

These are qualities reflected in my past and the Gallup Talent DNA Assessment (recent) and I know you want in your XXXX Salesforce. I want to bring these qualities to your sales staff. When may we plan a personal meeting?

Thank you for taking time to read this cover letter, I look forward to all further discussion.

All the Best,
XXXX XXXXXX

As I share these reader examples, I recommend that you get a highlighter and identify all the RESULTS. I'm sharing these exactly as they were given to me. See if you can figure out what they could have done better. For example, look at the first bullet above:

- *Our salespeople have infectious energy and enthusiasm resulting in sales of $1.4 Million.*

I highlighted the result. First of all, the way this was written is our natural way to communicate because we have been conditioned to start with WHAT. But after reading Part One, you know this is not the most powerful way to get a reader's attention. And how quickly did sales result in $1.4 million? Was that total sales or per salesperson? Was it in a quarter, a year, or longer? How would you re-write this? How about:

- *Our sales have increased by $1.4 million per salesperson, per year because we only hire salespeople that have an infectious energy and enthusiasm that our client's love.*

If you'd like to see another example, please read my bio in the back of this book.

Next, take a look at your own resume and cover letter and start highlighting the results. I'm betting that you have fewer results listed than you should. So take an hour of so and go give your most important professional documents a "Visnostic Facelift!" Even if you aren't looking for a job...you will feel really good about yourself when you start researching and listing more RESULTS.

I worked with a young man that tried hard to convince me that Visnostics would not work on his resume because he was no longer in a sales role. He was currently in a support role and he insisted that there were no results that he could identify. Needless to say, he said the wrong thing to the wrong person!

Again – **VISNOSTICS IS A THOUGHT PROCESS!** I challenged him to call someone in accounting, call someone that carried a quota for his accounts, and any other person that knew how much his clients were paying annually. I even suggested that the next time he talked with the clients, ask THEM what monetary (RTH) value, if any, they perceived that he provided.

As we all know, when clients are happy, they continue to pay their vendors. When they are unhappy and receive poor support, they will leave! So many employees do not see their own value and therefore, can't articulate that value on a resume. But put yourself in the hiring manager's shoes. He or she is trying to translate resumes into "How is this person going to make MY job easier and make ME more successful?" As with clients, you must do this translation for them or risk being thrown into the "round filing cabinet" because your resume hurts their brains!

Most resumes are terrible because most employees don't realize that they are ambassadors for their company and are "selling" the company to their clients every single day!

This young man called me back a couple of weeks later with some pretty impressive financial details and he also had a new attitude and appreciation for the job he was doing!

Until this Visnostic exercise required him to go looking for results, he had no idea that what he did was actually generating millions of dollars annually for his company!

Now that he had the RT data for the RTH formula, he was able to convert his resume from being very task (aka "H") focused and made it much more impactful by adding the results and timeline (aka RT) in front of what already existed. Take a good look at the resume and highlight the "results." They are at the beginning of each bullet.

Not only did he inspire himself to add these content improvements to his resume, he also was surprised how much better he felt about himself and he actually fell more in love with his job because he suddenly realized the value in what he did.

This positive attitude made him want to COSMETICALLY be more **VIS**ual in his resume too! The transformation in his resume was remarkable! He eventually converted this version of his resume to a Curriculum Vitae (CV) format that also includes charts, his photo, and other graphics. I am not sharing that version here to protect his privacy.

████████████████

██████████████████████

WORK EXPERIENCE:

Premier Account Specialist ████████ 3/14/17-Current
- ████ spends $1,457,933 annually on Platinum Support as a result of our daily engagements.
- My 17 implementations yield $2,023,000 in annual spend on Premier Support.
- Elected by peers to receive the ██████████████████ Award for Product Support FY19.
- Attended 30% more on-site meetings than any other rep in the org.
- Elected Leader for multiple Support Teams in FY19.
- Consistently Exceeding Standard stats for all tracked metrics.
- Selected as Chief Fun Officer for ██████████████, building community and culture in the Austin Office.

Sales Area Manager ████████ 7/7/15-10/1/16
- Initiated $416,537 investment made in Q2 FY16 by ██████████████ as a result of POC for Executive Team.
- Closed $271,510 in revenue resulting in $738,605 total income for the business by landed 50 net new logos.
- 7% response rate resulting from LinkedIn Campaign. Named Team's Leading Social Seller.
- 2 time VP Club award winner through quota attainment.
- Expertise in Healthcare, Education, and Commercial with +1000 Employees and under $1B Revenue.

Associate Sales Representative ████████ 6/7/14-7/1/15
- 38% increase in meetings scheduled from "California Natural Disaster Relief" campaign.
- Presented with the "First Impression" award, 1 of 30 individuals recognized of the 200 new hires.
- Enhanced speaking skills through Toastmasters Club Membership.
- Developed team-building skills/morale by coordinating team meetings, events, and mentoring new team members.

Video Producer ████████ 2011-2014
- 16% of support calls reduced by creating instructional tutorials.
- Directly reporting to Visioneer CFO, headed collaboration between Xerox Marketing and Visioneer business units.

EDUCATION:

████ **Sales Training** Seattle, WA 6/14-7/14

- The Skip Miller and John Barrows Training furthered my sales techniques.
- Formal training in one of the most desired skillsets in today's marketplace.

████ **Sales Academy** Burlingame, CA 6/14-7/14

- The Sandler Sales Methodology and Costigan Training enhanced my sales skills.
- Educated in IT from applications to database to storage and more.

The University of ████ ████████ 2011-2013

- Graduated with a 3.325/4.0 GPA.
- University Honors and Dean's List both recognized me as an outstanding student.
- Beta Upsilon Chi (Brothers Under Christ) Pledge Class President and Chair Member.

I hope you noticed that while resumes are not the typical Visnostic Statements requiring three responses, if you follow the same THOUGHT process, your resumes WILL be more impactful!

The hiring manager won't necessarily even know why they like your resume more than the hundred others they are flipping through. But by putting those results FIRST, you will make their review so much more pleasant because they won't have to translate what you do into why they will benefit from having you on their team!

Therefore, leveraging Visnostics while writing resumes and cover letters are an excellent example proving that Visnostics are not just about the statements...

VISNOSTICS ARE A THOUGHT PROCESS!

RTH =

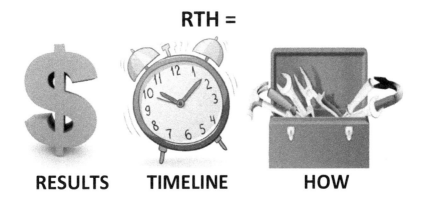

RESULTS   TIMELINE   HOW

SUCCESS THREE
PROSPECTING

I have several excellent examples of how readers are using Visnostics in their prospecting but I'm going to include those in the Website section since those efforts were used in phone scripts and emails. Instead, I'm going to show you how I am getting invited for speaking engagements and interviews on some incredible podcasts:

A few things that I hope you look for in your own communications are:

1. Subject is about THEM, not me or what I can do.
2. I don't talk about what I do or who I am in the first few paragraphs because the point is to get the reader to REFLECT on themselves, not what YOU want to accomplish!
3. Note that I intentionally bold the RESULTS and underline the TIMELINE. Do your bullets or points follow this format?

_____

Subject : Increasing Your Podcast Audience

"My Podcast audience increases every day because it features new and unique sales approaches nobody else covers!"

Please chose a response:
I WISH I could say this today!
I CAN say this today! (Score yourself 1 - 5 with 1 meaning it could be much better and 5 meaning you nailed it and there is no room for improvement.) or

213

This isn't important to me.

If you answered I WISH or scored yourself 1-4, let's make that statement a reality!

I was recently interviewed by Dr. Pelè and Brian Burns about the fundamentals of Visnostic Selling. Here are links to the recordings for your convenience:
https://www.youtube.com/watch?v=FbW-sSu4BOo

https://www.stitcher.com/podcast/brian-burns/the-brutal-truth-about-sales-selling/e/61931321

There are additional topics that are really resonating with my readers that you could be the first to explore.
Some examples for your consideration:

1. **Increase your sales** instantly by constructing stronger messaging (Using Visnostic's RTH).
2. **Establish client rapport** immediately using Visnostics to translate Features and Functions into "Client-Speak."
3. **Build sales confidence** during your podcast by sharing Visnostic reader Success Stories.
4. **Improve communication** in just 3 seconds with clients by understanding it's not WHAT you say, it's HOW you say it!
5. **Dramatically change salespeople's thought process** in just 30 minutes by understanding the Visnostic methodology.
6. **Improve internal relationships** in a DAY by leveraging Visnostic Team building for Sales & Marketing.

I look forward to discussing how these topics can increase both our businesses!

Happy Selling,

Kimberlee Slavik
CEO Dynamic Executives & Author of Visnostic Selling
kimslavik@dynaexec.com
214.532.XXXX cell
817.329.XXXX office
www.linkedin.com/in/kimslavik

_____

One of my newest readers is also a sales trainer and he believes strongly in providing videos in his prospecting emails. I actually find myself watching every single one he sends me. It feels so much more personal.

So the short, three minute website video that readers created to replace all the words and photos on my website, is also an excellent video to share while prospecting! https://player.vimeo.com/video/353714183.

If you're interested in having your own video created using Visnostics, they believe in Visnostics so passionately, that they have started the first Visnostic Video company!

Check them out at - http://neuroviews.com

And finally, one more example of how I prospect. I will write what appears to be a blog but it's much shorter than a typical blog. I try and incorporate as many neuroscience techniques as possible, such as using color, cartoons, and of course, Visnostic Statements. Here is one that I posted for an HR focused audience. My objective was to appeal to them to help me find temporary sales leadership roles.

While I enjoy training people and conducting workshops, my real passion is temporary sales leadership. Fractional Sales Leadership should be a much bigger business than it is today and I'm hoping Visnostics will help me accomplish this.

Attention Recruiters - Can you say this today?

Why place a candidate ONCE when you could place that same candidate multiple times every year???

Contact Kimberlee Slavik for details! #VisnosticSelling #DynaExec #FractionalSalesLeadership

How can YOU leverage this approach too?

SUCCESS FOUR
TRANSLATING WEBSITES

This has been a very interesting area for Visnostics because website development has been my weakest area professionally yet there is such a huge need to improve website content.

I know for a fact that my original website has COST me clients and I know that many companies have this same problem. In fact, Michael Bosworth told me that he almost didn't write my Foreword after seeing how hypocritical my website was and I don't blame him at all! Bosworth believes there is a fortune to be made converting websites into Visnostic Masterpieces of Story Telling. And he is right!

The magnitude of how horrible my website was is actually quite embarrassing but I couldn't make myself delete it until recently! The content was very Visnostic but Visnostic content is not enough. Unfortunately, I broke several of my own fundamental rules:

1. **It was overwhelmingly full of words versus graphics and what few graphics I had, didn't tie back to my message; they were just business stock photos.**
2. **It was full of photos and had zero cartoons and our brains prefer cartoons.**
3. **It was static and Visnostics teach us that our brains prefer movement such as videos.**
4. **It was full of bullets and didn't tell a very good story.**

I suspect that many readers can say the same thing about their current websites! The good news is that several of my readers came to my rescue and inspired me to let them translate my own website into a Visnostic Cartoon Video! In just three minutes, this new video summarizes what I so poorly attempted to communicate on my webpage using photos and way too many WORDS; the two things Visnostics preaches AGAINST!

When I compare my old website to this video, the general messaging is the same but is told very differently. Where have I heard that before...?

"It's not what we say, it's HOW we say it!"

However, I'm not done yet; the transformation is still underway.

Here is an example of the graphics originally used on DynaExec.com. This is also the original wording before it was converted to Client-Speak.

This content was replaced with the following three minute video - https://player.vimeo.com/video/353714183. Here is the actual script and some graphic samples from the storyboard:

Hi! I'm Kimberlee Slavik, CEO of DynaExec.

CLIENT-SPEAK SELLING WITH VISNOSTICS

During my thirty successful years in sales and sales leadership, I've been forced to overcome the same challenges regardless of the size of company I represented.

CLIENT-SPEAK SELLING WITH VISNOSTICS

I finally documented my secrets so you, your team, and your clients can say the following statements about YOUR sales and marketing:

Hi! My name is Sam and I am in marketing.

CLIENT-SPEAK SELLING WITH
VISNOSTICS

Sales have increased 40% this quarter because our marketing team no longer creates messaging around our features and functions."

CLIENT-SPEAK SELLING WITH
VISNOSTICS

Brand new salespeople are confident and competent to be in front of clients from their first week on the job because marketing has created a powerful tool that helps guide a client conversation without needing much product knowledge.

My name is Mike. I'm the Vice President of Sales.

CLIENT-SPEAK SELLING WITH
VISNOSTICS

Sales are exceeding monthly revenue objectives because marketing has stopped giving us the typical presentations and brochures full of jargon, buzz words, and generic sounding marketing fluff. Instead, they have TRANSLATED what we DO into a language our clients understand and love!

CLIENT-SPEAK SELLING WITH VISNOSTICS

Our company is more profitable because new salespeople can quickly and easily learn how to communicate what we sell.

I LOVE our marketing team because we have aligned our priorities and have learned how to be successful together!

_____

Hi there. I'm Karen and I'm the leader of all the technical talent in my company.

Our sales team is competent and confident enough to carry on an intelligent technical conversation with potential clients without us; which means my team's time is no longer wasted early in the sales cycle!

CLIENT-SPEAK SELLING WITH VISNOSTICS

Our technical meetings with clients are far more productive because we now have time to properly prepare and help our salespeople close deals later in the sales cycle.

_____

Hi I'm Tony and I'm a very happy client.

CLIENT-SPEAK SELLING WITH VISNOSTICS

Mike and his sales team translated their features and functions into a vision of how I could use them so I didn't have to.

Mike really understands my pains and he has become an extension of my own team! No other salesperson has ever accomplished this!

I used to buy from vendors based on price. But today I won't even talk to the competition because I don't understand their marketing message.

CLIENT-SPEAK SELLING WITH VISNOSTICS

AND none of them seem to be in the same league as Mike and his team.

Hey it's Kimberlee again.

Wouldn't you LOVE to experience the same successes as Sam, Mike, Karen and Tony?

CLIENT-SPEAK SELLING WITH VISNOSTICS

To learn more about the benefits of translating VENDOR-Speak into CLIENT-Speak using Visnostics, contact me directly at either LinkedIn or here at DynaExec.

I am so proud of this father/daughter team of Paul Chiumento and Katie Russell because everything about their brand new business, NeuroViews was inspired by *Visnostic Selling.*

They actually made that video for me and I am so touched and so grateful! And their company is the first one that I'm aware of that is 100% Visnostic focused! If you missed it in the Prospecting chapter, here is their brand new company and website again - http://neuroviews.com.

And they actually have several other companies that they have completely converted to Visnostic language, visuals, and formats described in this book! Also check out www.infinityearnings.biz and www.ffil.biz.

Another reader, Gary Metz of Ingenious Geeks was inspired about the short attention spans mentioned in *Visnostic Selling* and he created a seven second video for me summarizing Visnostics. You can view it on the DynaExec website or on YouTube - https://www.youtube.com/watch?v=dy5s4kYWdjY.

Michael Bosworth was the fastest execution of Visnostics that I've seen! He stopped reading the draft of my original book after Chapter One because he was compelled to immediately start revising his training content! I am so honored that he wrote my Foreword for *Visnostic Selling* and he wrote a brand new Foreword for *Visnostic Sales and Marketing*! This second Foreword is so exciting to me because it demonstrates just how quickly he is becoming an expert with Visnostics; which means you can too!

The newest Foreword in this book mentions his company, Story Seekers https://www.customerheroselling.com and his wife, Jennifer Lehr's online marriage counseling company, WeConcile. https://www.weconcile.com.

I hope you take time to explore the content on Jennifer's website because it is the most impressive execution of Visnostics on a website that I've seen so far!

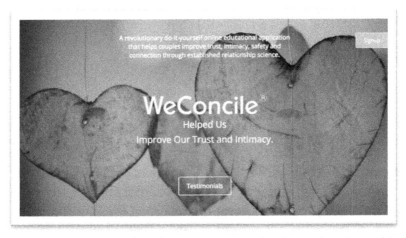

While Mike immediately incorporated Visnostics into his extremely successful training content, he hasn't started incorporating Visnostics on his website yet.

However, his wife's use of Visnostics on her website is brilliant. Please take the time to check out her assessment quiz Here are a few screen shots so you can why I am so impressed with her execution of the Visnostic approach:

Try it out! Her quiz is so clean and simple to take!

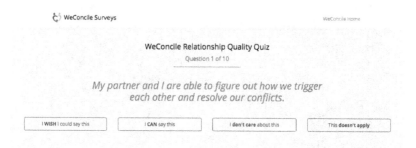

I love her version of the "I CAN Say This Today" along with her scoring options! This is such a great example how readers can modify Visnostics to make them perfect for your specific audience! Check out the drop-down options:

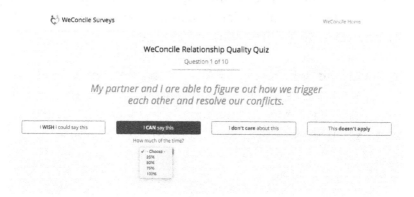

We prefer to see things that are not static. Earlier, I used video as an example of a non-static visual. However, even static photos can be made "less static." For example, do you have photos of your products or do you have photos of people USING your products?

One of my childhood buddies, Tony Duran has a successful business manufacturing all types of QUALITY booths. Here are some of his websites:

http://www.boothsforu.com
http://www.nostalgiawarehouse.com
http://www.arlingtonredliners.com
http://www.cityviewstation.com

BEFORE Visnostics, his graphics were static; it was all about the booths. AFTER reading Visnostics, he hired a professional photographer and rounded up some models to help potential clients VISUALIZE people having FUN in his booths. While his websites are currently under construction, I got to be at one of his photo shoots and he shared some of the new photos so I could include them in this chapter.

Here is a current (BEFORE) photo of his booths from his current website and the photo on the right is the replacement photo (AFTER)– You can see the HUGE difference when you help your audience visualize how they may "feel" with your product!

To say that I am proud and honored to meet my readers, interact with them, get to know them, and LEARN from them is an understatement. Dozens of strangers are quickly becoming dear friends as we help and support each other grow with Visnostics.

This is, by far, the most rewarding thing I have ever done professionally. THANK YOU!

What blows my mind is that this second edition of Visnostic Selling was under development just three months after the original release! THAT is how fast people are executing, sharing, and seeing results from Visnostics!

I look forward to hearing from more of you very soon!

And stay tuned! My new Visnostic Website will be up and running as soon as I finish writing all these books! My priority is always to help others FIRST.

"When you help others be successful, your own success will become a natural RESULT!"

~ Me

SUCCESS FIVE
VERTICAL SUCCESS – REAL ESTATE

Out of over 14 million salespeople in the world today, Real Estate Agents and Auto Salespeople comprise a huge percentage of that number.

In addition, several early readers told me that they questioned if Visnostics would work as well with B2C (Business to Consumer/Customer) Sales as it did in my career, which focused on B2B (Business to Business) Sales.

So it didn't take me long to justify writing "Special Edition" Visnostic books for those two specific careers. I'm including excerpts from both those books because they are full of reader successes and have incredible examples of Visnostic execution.

The Real Estate Version became a best seller and the Foreword was written by Denise Fair, the owner of RE/MAX in Waco, Texas. Denise has a strong passion for Visnostics because she saw its power almost immediately. She shared with me one of my favorite success stories:

There was a very generic house that had been on the market for six months with a real estate agency and it had very few showings and no offerings. Needless to say, when the contract on the original listing expired, the sellers went with another agency and it just happened to be awarded to one of the readers of *Visnostic Selling*.

This new agent published a "Coming Soon" ad with a photo of the house but instead of stating the usual number of bedrooms and bathrooms, the caption went something like this:

I can walk to the boat ramp and take a relaxing ride on the lake after a long day at the office. I don't have to worry when the kids are playing in the backyard because the swimming pool has a secure safety fence separating it from the fun and colorful playground. And mornings are a breeze with the spacious kitchen that gives us all plenty of room to grab breakfast while lunches are prepared on the huge island. The open floor plan has the perfect place for a Christmas tree yet plenty of room for the entire family to gather and roast marshmallows in the fire-burning fireplace.

This is the perfect dream house for a busy young family to make lasting memories. If you wish you could say this about YOUR home, come to the open house this Saturday...blah blah blah...

When the new listing agent arrived 15 minutes prior to the open house, she was pleasantly surprised to see several people already in line! The house received multiple offers that first day and sold for $30,000 over the asking price!

Remember, this same house was listed with another agent for six months with very few viewings and no offers. The original agent advertised the old fashioned way by leading with square footage and the number of bedrooms and bathrooms.

But that's not all! The new listing agent signed three more listings because several people that saw the advertisement wanted her to market their homes the same way!

Why do you think you need to talk square footage, number of bedrooms, and number of bathrooms?

Just like the moral in the "Roast Story," don't just do it that way because that's the way everybody else does it. Why not get more scientific and help your potential buyers actually ENJOY the buying experience? You may even enjoy your job more too!

As you can imagine, I have been talking about these principles to many people with various careers. I had a Real Estate Agent friend of mine say that this doesn't apply to their business because clients buy homes based upon the number of bedrooms and bathrooms. I thought that was an interesting perspective. The best Real Estate Agent I ever met told me that she didn't sell homes she sold dreams. She sold us two homes and not once did we discuss the number of bedrooms or bathrooms. Instead, she asked me to describe how I envisioned living in my next home.

I explained that our friends lost all of their children in a fire because all the kids were upstairs and the master was downstairs. I told her I would like the downstairs to have a nice flow for entertaining but that I preferred all the bedrooms be located upstairs. I described wanting to wake up in the mornings and step out on the balcony that overlooked a pool. I wanted fireplaces downstairs but I thought a fireplace in the master bedroom was romantic. I told her that I didn't care about the kitchen because I prefer to eat out but that I wanted a breakfast area to drink coffee and look at the pool. I explained that my husband and I both needed offices away from each other. I told her that I loved the look of a spiraling staircase but that wasn't mandatory. As I described these things to her, I felt emotional and anxious while I wondered if my perfect dream home even existed.

Well, it did exist. It was the first and only house she showed us and it was nothing like we imagined. It was a Georgian Style and that wasn't something we thought we wanted. When we pulled up, my husband didn't even want to go inside. But the Agent talked us into taking a look because she said she thought we would be surprised. As we walked through the house, my husband was unimpressed with the colors and the style. But I realized she was showing me my exact description! She did a great job bringing my thoughts to the surface so as I walked through the house, those thoughts were already on my mind and I was able to help my husband see the home's potential. I instantly imagined how we would live in the house. I never even noticed how many bedrooms. For the record, it had five but two of them became offices. We bought this house in 2000 and have lived in our dream home ever since.

Do you realize all the time and inconvenience this agent managed to avoid for **all** concerned? She was brilliant for asking me to describe how I wanted to **live in the house** instead of asking **how many bedrooms or bathrooms we THOUGHT we wanted.** This quick sell gave her more time to show more homes to more people. If we ever sell, she will be the first one I call because I know there won't be a lot of unnecessary strangers in our home.

I see Real Estate ads all the time that describe the number of bedrooms and the number of bathrooms along with a picture of a home and its square footage.

If we had seen an elevation of our current home with a description of five bedrooms and four bathrooms, we would have never agreed to look at it!

So do ads that start off with the number of bedrooms and bathrooms really do an effective job attracting the right buyers to the right homes?

Our Agent did us a great service by asking how we envisioned living in the home versus asking us what features and functions we THOUGHT we wanted. By doing this, she triggered emotions that I didn't even know I had! She was using neuroscience before I even knew what it was!

3 BEDROOM, 2 BATH HOME AND 30X40 SHOP FOR SALE IN WASHINGTON SCHOOL DISTRICT ON 2.4 ACRES

POSTED ON MAY 28, 2019 BY DEBORAH

Sweet little home that's neat as a pen, on rural acreage with no restrictions! 2.4 acres is fenced on all 3 sides... has a nice 30X40 metal shop with RV hookup, concrete floor, has electric and plumbed for water and sewer. Good production water well and City Water Tap is installed, but not in use. All this in the Washington School District! What are you waiting for!

Is this what your home ads look like? What if someone just needs one bedroom but two offices? Are the bedrooms, bathrooms, and square footage descriptions you share forcing your potential clients to TRANSLATE how they would use it?

The advertisement above says this house is in the Washington School District. Is that a good thing? Your potential client may need to go do research to find out why that is important. And since we just learned in Part One that people avoid making that extra effort, will they ignore the ad and keep looking? Did the author of this listing assume all potential buyers would automatically know that Washington School District is a selling point?

Now read the description again; it says "rural acreage with no restrictions." Why is that important? Is it because there are no HOA dues? But does it also mean that my neighbors can have a stinky and noisy pig farm next door? Again, each person is going to translate that into something that they can relate to and **it won't always be a good thing**. This form of advertising is dangerous because you have no idea if your audience is interpreting your points as a positive or negative attribute of the home!

I challenge you to rewrite the captions using a Visnostic style to guide your reader to a positive conclusion.

Reader Story – David Stoltzman – Randy White Real Estate Services

I was working with a young man that just started in the real-estate business and he read *Visnostic Selling* and really embraced it. One of the chapters dives deep into what I call "Segmentation." This is when you reflect on your different types of audiences and determine how you can categorize your message to each of their specific priorities.

First of all, how does a Real Estate Agent choose to be with one agency over another? So one of the segmentation groups should contain Visnostic Statements geared towards **recruiting** the best talent to your agency.

Then once you are staffed up, you will want to attract potential **clients that want to sell** their homes. This will build an inventory of homes to sell. And once you have listings, you will want to **appeal to the actual Buyers**.

This young man was new but he is sharp and he pointed out that a fourth segmentation is needed that would be written for **both Buyers and Sellers**.

Here are the Visnostic Statements this future Real Estate Super-Star sent me after reading just the first chapter of *Visnostic Selling*:

SELLERS -

Please choose one of these three responses to each statement below.

- **I can say this today!**
- **I WISH I could say this today!**
  or
- **It's not important, not applicable, or I don't know.**

I know exactly what price my home would sell for today.
I am aware of what I will net at closing when I sell my home.
I already have my next home picked out.
I have a timeline for when I want to sell and be in my next home.
My home is the top-viewed home on Zillow for my neighborhood.
My home is ready to be photographed and is staged appropriately for marketing.
My home could sell for top-dollar in its current condition.
I desire a hands-off, resort-like experience when selling my home.
If I am not satisfied with my Agent's performance + communication, I want the option to cancel our agreement.

What other statements would you say that were omitted?

BUYERS -

Please choose one of these three responses to each statement below.

- **I can say this today!**
- **I WISH I could say this today!**
  or
- **It's not important, not applicable, or I don't know.**

I know the home buying process in Texas from beginning to end.
My Agent only shows me homes in my criteria, or I request to see.
My Agent doesn't obligate or "hard sell" me on a particular home.
My Agent points out minor and major cosmetic/material flaws in every home we see.
I receive comps on every home I consider offering on, so I don't over-extend.
My Agent has an "off-market" list, and reaches out to other agents for "coming soon" listings.
I'm confident I know what my closing costs will be on buying a home.
I don't feel nervous or anxious about buying a home.
I can effectively forecast appreciation for each home I see.

What other statements would you say that were omitted?

BUYERS AND SELLERS –

Please choose one of these three responses to each statement below.

- **I can say this today!**
- **I WISH I could say this today!**
  or
- **It's not important, not applicable, or I don't know**

I have a trusted Agent-resource for my neighborhood.
My Agent has an extensive track record selling homes.
I communicate regularly with my current Real Estate-resource.
I have other resources i.e. local lenders, licensed contractors, inspectors, and other top professionals.
I feel comfortable navigating the TREC contract, addendums, amendments, disclosures, title docs and survey.
I can confidently negotiate on my behalf what is important to me in a real estate transaction.
My Agent communicates with us on nights and weekends, if needed.
I know how to interpret a closing disclosure so I know who pays for what in a transaction.
I know the tangible and intangible factors that drive home prices in my area.

What other statements would you say that were omitted?

And then finally, what if you owned an agency and you wanted to recruit top talent? What types of Visnostic Statements would differentiate your agency from the competition?

The Visnostic Statements David created are exceptionally good, especially for someone that has never thought this way or articulated a message by leveraging visualizations.

However, two chapters from Part One were dedicated to helping you write the absolute best and strongest statements possible.

Because David is with Randy White Real Estate Services, I decided to go explore randywhite.com. This is something you can do as well to assess your own marketing. Most potential clients are going to do exactly what I'm doing; I'm looking for results and timelines in his client testimonials. I need to "translate" what is on his website. "Why should I care about what is stated on his website." "How is this agency better than the others?" "What is in it for me?"

Results almost always answer these questions and differentiate one company from all the others.

I'm going to paste the first three testimonials I see and demonstrate what to look for when creating the strongest Visnostic Statements.

Example #1 – Read this and look for RESULTS and TIMELINE.

"We have known Randy White for many years and have had the good fortune to have him as our Agent on two separate occasions. Randy is a true professional who knows his business and the market inside and out, and has given us excellent advice always. He and his team, Brenda and Teresa, are great to work with, extremely responsive and are always looking out for our best interests. Aside from the fact that Randy just sold our house quickly and efficiently, this team is a true pleasure to work with. All around it is a win to work with Randy White!"

Here is some additional coaching before you review the other examples:

Because results and timelines are important to clients, they tend to naturally mention them but sometimes you will have to dig for them. In this example, the seller didn't get to the result until the very end of the recommendation. Unfortunately, most people will stop reading before they get to those results. But with some minor coaching, the seller could turn this into a really impactful referral by just moving some words around.

Also remember that we are so conditioned to believe WHAT someone does is a result, that it's normal to overlook the actual RESULT of what they do. For example, "Randy is a true professional" is what he does. "Answering all their questions" is a result of his professional demeanor but it's still something he does. Refer back to the beginning of the book when I described symptoms and causes and how a doctor has to be careful not to attempt to treat a symptom. The Doctor will need to diagnose the cause before he or she can properly treat the patient.

In Visnostics, the thought process is similar; Randy is professional but the result is that he sold their house quickly. He gave excellent advice but the result from that advice is that the house sold quickly. You can give great advice and be professional all day long and still not sell a house. So we can assume that something Randy is doing is more effective than other Real Estate Professionals. We need to flush out what that is to differentiate him from all the other people trying to sell homes. **Visnostics is a thought process because you will begin to view your marketing wording very differently once you learn what to look for what clients really care about.**

"...has given us excellent advice" is really what the Agent DID. What resulted from the good advice? Saved money? Sold house faster? Because we aren't making any claims, we are going to take some liberties here to develop a sample statement. However, finding these types of incomplete results and/or timelines is a great excuse to go back to the client and try and flush out these details.
Timeline – "always"
(the more precise timeline given, the better the quality of the Visnostics)

Results mentioned – "Randy sold our house" (efficiently)
Timeline – "quickly"

242

(It would be nice to know specifically how quickly. Was it a day? Week? Month?)

Example #2 –

"We met Randy White in 1994 and instantly knew we would have a great relationship with him. He has helped us sell and buy three homes since we met him. Randy has always been positive in listing our homes and that they would sell quickly. His extensive knowledge of the real estate business is why we always trusted him in listing our homes. His office personnel are just as positive and knowledgeable as he is. Any questions or concerns were quickly answered by Randy or his assistant. We support and recommend him and his staff to anyone who has real estate needs."

Results mentioned – "sell and buy three homes"
Timeline – "1994…since we met him"

Results mentioned – "they would sell"
Timeline – "quickly"

Example # 3 –

"Randy was wonderful to work with and is very knowledgeable about the metroplex market. His office staff were always easy to speak with and quick to return our phone calls or emails when necessary. The process went as smoothly as it could have in today's uncertain economy."

Results mentioned – this one omitted the results. We can't even tell if this recommendation is from a Buyer or a Seller. It's assumed that their house sold or they bought a home. It was very focused on the "WHAT" they did to make it a good experience versus what were the desired outcome/results.
Timeline – "always" "quick"

So out of the first three recommendations I reviewed, two were fairly strong and one was complimentary but the outcome could be clearer.

VERY IMPORTANT POINT - This Visnostic Statement creation process is a powerful exercise. Looking for results and timelines will open your eyes to why some marketing "feels" better than others.

Are you starting to see how your thought process is already changing? Once you know what to look for, you will view previous recommendations very differently.

Once you embrace the Visnostic Communication Style, you may want to go back to the clients that provided recommendations and ask them to add these additional details. You will find that most people will be eager to make those enhancements for you.

So now let me show you the Visnostic Statements we can create from these three client testimonials:

Always try and start with the RESULTS and then the TIMELINE. You may be surprised how difficult this is to do because of how conditioned we are to start with the HOW in our sentences.

REMEMBER that our attention spans are down to 3 seconds. That means your first three words better be powerful for the reader to even consider continuing with your message. The best way to catch attention is by putting results first.

"I saved a million dollars" is much more powerful when it was saved in a month versus ten years. Which is why including a timeline is very important to include in your statements.

Visnostic Statements from Exercises 1, 2, & 3 above are:

1. **Randy sold two of our homes quickly due to his professionalism, his efficient team, and his knowledge of the industry.**
2. **Randy has helped us buy and sell three homes since 1994 due to his extensive knowledge of the real estate business and his positive and knowledgeable team.**
3. **Not enough information to create a Visnostic Statement. This one just praised his performance. We have no idea if they even sold or bought a home.**

Here is another way to word them and present them. Can you tell which of these are for Sellers and which are for Buyers?

Please choose one of these three responses to each statement below.

- **I can say this today!**
- **I WISH I could say this today!**
  or
- **It's not important, not applicable, or I don't know**

Our Agent <u>sold</u> our house <u>quickly</u>. (Seller)
We <u>saved thousands of dollars</u> thanks to <u>always</u> receiving excellent advice from our Agent. (Unknown)
We have <u>bought or sold three homes</u> in <u>25 years</u> with the same Agent. (Buyer AND Seller)
The entire selling and buying experience was <u>always</u> <u>enjoyable</u> because the entire team was so <u>responsive</u> to our needs. (Buyer AND Seller)

These are very good Visnostic Statements but I went back to the references in an attempt to find a dream recommendation.

I want to create a GREAT Visnostic Statement for this real estate section and I found a really good one that was buried! In fact, this one is so good that if I were Randy, I would put THIS recommendation FIRST on my webpage!

As you read through this recommendation, try and find all the timelines first.

Timelines are usually complementary to a result.

<u>**EXAMPLE #4**</u> – Best Source for Visnostic Statements

"We have worked with Randy over the last 15 years or so in all our personal real estate transactions. He has acted as our agent/broker on three different properties of ours. In all cases Randy was always of the utmost integrity, completeness of task, acted in the best interest of all parties, gathered our requirements accurately and never put any unnecessary pressure on us to do something we did not want to do. He is a true professional and I would recommend Randy to anyone I know or don't know. One most important factor I do not want to miss is, his knowledge of the markets, and understanding how to price homes to sell them is outstanding. (IE) In all three transactions where he sold our properties for us he sold them and had a contract on all of them in less than one week when the market was running at 100 days plus to contract. In summary, Randy White is a true professional, and no matter in the future whatever real estate transactions we are involved in, you can count on it that we will be securing Randy White to handle them for us!! "

Results – sold our (3) properties

Before I write the Visnostic Statement, I want to point out that there is a ton of positive feedback here. But think like the client, not like an agent. You may find this is extremely difficult to do.

Timeline – 15 years, in less than one week.

Almost all of these recommendations declared Randy White as a very knowledgeable professional. That is great. However, the potential buyer or seller has to translate that into "Why do I care about this?" "What is the benefit to me?" "Everybody says they are professional so I still don't understand why he is different." YOU MUST DO THIS TRANSLATION FOR YOUR CLIENTS!

The answer they are looking for are usually in the results.

It's also good to differentiate buyer recommendations from seller recommendations because your audience has one of those two things on his or her mind when trying to make a decision. We need to stop making clients do this translation. We must start doing it for them. With that said, here is the GREAT Visnostic Statement I was able to build for this real estate focused book:

My Real Estate Agent had a contract on all three of my homes in less than a week when all the other Agents were averaging 100 days or more!

This Visnostic Statement is so good, that I HAD to put it on the back cover of the Real Estate Special Edition!

This is a powerful SELLER Visnostic Statement because any potential Sellers now know that the person writing this recommendation was not just a lucky sale; this Agent sold THREE of his homes in less than a week! This recommendation finally did a fantastic job differentiating Randy White from the other agents out there by including the additional information about average sales taking 100 days.

Who wouldn't respond with
"I WISH I COULD SAY THAT TODAY?!"

SUCCESS SIX
VERTICAL SUCCESS – AUTO SALES

How many automotive salespeople do you think there are in the United States?

I don't know either but it's not from lack of trying! Per NADA (National Automobile Dealers Association), The nation's 16,753 franchised dealers sold 17.22 million light-duty **vehicles**. Total new-**vehicle** sales topped $1 trillion. Dealerships wrote more than 310 million repair orders, with service and parts sales totaling more than $116 billion.

But that is just automobiles. What about jet skis, boats, forklifts, cargo vans, big rigs, or motorcycles, just to name a few.

As I was researching, I did happen to uncover the Guinness Book of World Record's Top Salesperson - Joseph Samuel Girardi, **better** known as Joe Girard, (November 1, 1928 - February 28, 2019) was an American **salesman**. Girard sold 13,001 **cars** at a Chevrolet dealership between 1963 and 1978, and was recognized by the Guinness Book of World Records as the seller of the most **cars** in a year (1,425 in 1973).

So let's just say that a LOT of people are making a LOT of money selling things with engines.

What's crazy is that most of them are selling them all wrong! Hard to believe – right? Imagine how many more autos they would sell if they started doing it RIGHT!

Try searching online for any vehicle and you will get statistics such as miles per gallon, engine type, available colors, horsepower, and tons of "technology" that have fancy trademarked names that us poor consumers have no clue what they mean.

However, when you ask someone why they bought their car or what they like about their car, the answers are very different.

Visnostics – Special Edition for Auto Sales was published August 2019 despite not having a Foreword because the need to get the information out there was so great.

Here is an excerpt from that book;

You should now be able to see how Visnostic Statements can strengthen your marketing content. What blows my mind is how difficult it is to change these bad behaviors!

There have been many books written throughout the years attempting to change or improve the ways products are marketed. Yet everybody continues to do it the same old way because, just like the "roast" story I told in the Introduction of this book, nobody questions it. Buyers don't question it and neither do the Sellers. If you want to be innovative, if you want to make a difference, why not try something new?

Remember, your competitors are reading this book as well! The "winner" will be the dealerships that embrace VISNOSTICS FIRST!

Visnostics destroy the insanity that is taking place with all the features and functions being advertised in an attempt to sell cars! I want to leave you with one final story:

I bought this car in 2001 with a pretty good commission check. And yes, I used Visnostics to win the business. I just didn't fully understand the science behind what I was doing yet.

Here is the original advertisement I saw online:

1966 AC Shelby Cobra hybrid (part replica/part original)
Air conditioning was added to the Cobra
1.1 k miles
Larry Lingenfelter built 390 cubic inch,
FE Block Tremec 5-speed
Flawless pearl blue and white stripes
Black leather embroidered seats imported from Italy
Boyd Coddington wheels
Ceramic coated headers and pipes
Chrome Aldan shocks

Complete engine dress kit

_____

Here is the story behind the car – my husband had Auto Trader magazines lying all around our house. One day, I flipped through one to see what types of cars he had dog-eared and I was appalled to see old muscle cars that needed a LOT of work. I envisioned our HOA flipping out when my husband ended up with one of these cars in our driveway, up on blocks. I envisioned oil stains everywhere and a stinky and grumpy husband frustrated as he tried to restore these classics to their glory. I also envisioned how expensive it was going to be and how long it was going to take. He obviously needed my help to find a GOOD car and keep our HOA from breathing down our necks!

So I went online and I found this beauty. It was gorgeous and I could tell it wasn't going to need any work done to it.

When my husband got home from work, I showed him this car and he said, "I have that car dog-eared!" And I said, "No you don't. I looked at all of your Auto Traders and I saw the cars you were looking at." He then pulled out a brand new Auto Trader from his brief case and it was true – he had it dog-eared. WE BOTH LOVED THIS CAR!

I don't know which one of us was more surprised but because of this unusual alignment in taste, we HAD to go look at this car!

I was so sure I was going to buy it that I got a cashier's check and we got a trailer and drove two hours to look at it.

When we actually saw it in person, the look on my husband's face was priceless. But when the owner started the car, I was stunned how my body physically reacted; I actually got goose bumps! No car had ever affected me like that! The base sound from the exhaust pipes took my breath away! I envisioned how cool we would look driving this beauty around town! SOLD!

We have now had this car for over 18 years! Oh my gosh! I just realized how crazy that is! We baby this car. It stays in a garage and is covered. We hardly drive it and I actually got up from writing this to go see what our mileage is on the car and I even took a picture just for this story.

This is going to make a lot of readers sick to see –

This car is obviously wasted on us! This means in 18 years, we have only driven this car 2,557.6 miles! That means we averaged about 142 miles per year. I am ashamed of us!

My husband said it sounds like it needs a new water pump so the past few times I've wanted to drive it, we can't. And other times I have wanted to drive it, the inspection or tags were expired. Which is why it's been sitting in the garage more than it's been on the road.

But when we DO get it out, WOW! First of all, every single time I drive it, my heart rate goes up because my adrenaline goes into over-drive. I have no idea why this happens. It hasn't happened with any other vehicle. I respect the power of this car. I won't even drink coffee if I'm going to drive it because I'm afraid I will have a heart attack!

When we drive it, people speed up to get next to us. We get dozens of "thumbs up" signs, people honk, wave, and SMILE! The biggest joy to me is how this car affects other people! It puts a huge smile on the faces of most people driving around us and I love that feeling.

One of our favorite things to do is to park the car in front of a restaurant patio, go eat on the patio and people-watch. What I LOVE to see is when people take pictures standing around it and we will walk up to them and open the door and tell them to get in and we offer to take pictures of them. They get so excited! And that is so fun for us! I love imagining all the pictures of this car that are posted on Instagram.

The reason that I just shared all of that in this book is to make my point about how to sell more autos! **NOT ONCE DID I EVER MENTION ANY OF THE THINGS IN THE ORIGINAL ADVERTISEMENT AS REASONS I LOVE THIS CAR OR WHY I BOUGHT IT!** So imagine how much more you could sell if you would stop selling like this:

1966 AC Shelby Cobra hybrid (part replica/part original)
Air conditioning was added to the Cobra
1.1 k miles
Larry Lingenfelter built 390 cubic inch,
FE Block Tremec 5-speed
Flawless pearl blue and white stripes
Black leather embroidered seats imported from Italy
Boyd Coddington wheels
Ceramic coated headers and pipes
Chrome Aldan shocks
Complete engine dress kit

I didn't even know what most of the stuff listed was or why I should care!

You will be shocked how many more calls you will get if you would paint a VISION of how your Buyer's life will be better. They will not only come to you, they will ASK you to sell to them! It is AFTER they come see you that you discuss all those Features and Functions. But only if and when they ASK!

I'm not saying that there's no NEED for the features and functions; **the problem is that salespeople and marketing rely on the Features and Functions and expect buyers to paint their visions in their head. But most of us are too lazy to do that! So we need to do it for them!**

Visnostics teaches to sell like THIS –

"You're feeling like a celebrity on this gorgeous 70 degree day; wind in your hair, people honking, waving, smiling, and taking pictures...You feel sexy, sassy, and FREE of any worries! Your adrenaline is flowing from the power of this maintenance free, brand new, 1966 AC Shelby Cobra you are driving. Life just doesn't get any better than this!"

Can YOU say this today?
Do you WISH you could say this today?
Or is it even important to you?
If you WISH you could say this today, call me at
XXX.XXX.XXXX!

Does this make sense? You may need to see it work to really understand the power of Visnostics!

SO WHEN ARE YOU GOING TO TRY IT?

This mini-lesson, written exclusively for Auto Sales Professionals, is intended to give you a taste of what to expect from any of the books in the Visnostic Series.

Visnostic Sales and Marketing will teach you how to create actual sales tools that **will ensure new salespeople are confident and competent to interact with clients From their first few days selling!**

To learn more about developing powerful Visnostic Statements, and how to work with your existing clients to create the absolute best testimonials, please read any of the Visnostic Series by Kimberlee Slavik. The books are available in over 42,000 bookstores worldwide.

For information about scheduling workshops or keynote speaking at any of your business meetings, please email autosales@dynaexec.com.

SUCCESS SEVEN
VERTICAL SUCCESS – MARKETING

When marketing and sales are in alignment, magic happens! I've been blessed to have worked with some incredible marketing professionals in my career and few things create a stronger bond than successful teamwork and collaboration.

I have known Omar Barraza for over ten years and he is one of those marketing people that I am proud to have worked with. Because this book is intended for both sales and marketing professionals, I wanted to be sure that marketing had the best representation as possible. So I asked Omar if he would consider co-writing a book with me. I'm not sure if this will end up being another Special Edition but it absolutely needs to be included in *Visnostic Sales and Marketing!*

By Omar Barraza,
Founder and Strategist at PlanStartGrow®

I rather vividly remember the day I met Kimberlee Slavik. She was introduced to me as a top sales talent with a background in the technology industry. Later that day I opened up LinkedIn and was a bit awe struck by her background and accomplishments.

The thing that caught my attention so many years ago, and continues true to this day, is that she is unique in the way she does things versus other sales executives. I suppose the key difference could be summarized in this way: while many sales executives operate as 'hunters' or 'farmers' or 'gatherers', Kimberlee is a customer and client 'magnet'.

Kimberlee explained to me how she does things years ago, but while reading her recent book, it became obvious that I hadn't begun to understand what she shared with me. If you are a marketer or familiar with the inbound marketing methodology, think of Kimberlee's approach as "inbound sales" where business people volunteer to become customers and clients.

Reviewing how Visnostics and marketing intersect and why this benefits marketers, customers, and clients is what this chapter is all about.

WHY VISNOSTICS HELPS MARKETERS

A key benefit of using Visnostics for marketing is prospective customers and clients do a lot of valuable marketing research and communications for you!

It's likely that most prospective clients and customers are interested in buying goods and services that address specific needs if they are businesses (business-to-business or B2B model) or wants if they are consumers (business-to-consumer or B2C model). A food equipment manufacturer needs to reduce production costs and purchases a machine that automates welding, for example, while a college student wants to lighten their campus backpack and buys a tablet to replace a notebook computer. This means accurately determining needs, wants, and expectations is vital to marketers and business success.

264

So how do you reveal needs, wants, and expectations? One way is it perform primary and secondary research of markets and competitors, current clients and customers, and relevant audiences. You might conduct one-to-one interviews as primary research to learn about manufacturer needs, and you might review social network as secondary research to learn about college student wants. Or, you could use Visnostics instead.

EXAMPLE ONE: Food Equipment Manufacturers

A vendor of automated welding machines could use the following Visnostic statements. Each statement would be presented to business leaders and relevant employees and then each person would be asked to choose the most relevant response.

Responses
- A – I can say this today!
- B – I wish I could say this today.
- C – It's not important, not applicable, or I don't know.

VISNOSTIC STATEMENTS: Food Equipment Manufacturers
We rarely loose a sales opportunity due to competitive pricing
My manufacturing facilities are as efficient as possible
I produce equipment at costs equal to or lower than competitors
The quality of our equipment cannot be further improved

VISNOSTIC STATEMENTS: Food Equipment Manufacturers
We never have welding injuries or downtime on the production floor

In this business-to-business example, the Visnostic Statements you choose for marketing automated welding machines should focus on revealing the most valuable needs and expectations of equipment manufacturers. Ideally, you would focus your statements to:

- Highlight aspirations such as improving quality
- Identify emotional issues such beating competitors
- Surface chronic problems such controlling costs

Think of three more Visnostic Statements relevant to this example and write them below.

VISNOSTIC STATEMENTS

EXAMPLE TWO: College Students

A retailer of personal electronics devices could use the following Visnostic Statements. Each statement would be presented to college students and then each person would be asked to choose the most relevant response.

Responses
- A – I can say this today!
- B – I wish I could say this today.
- C – It's not important, not applicable, or I don't know.

VISNOSTIC STATEMENTS: College Students
The computer I use for class notes, work, and tests works just like my smartphone
The computer I use for class notes, work, and tests is always connected to the Internet
The computer I use for class notes, work, and tests is very light and convenient to use
My notebook computer battery is always charged whenever I need to use it
There's a lot of unused space in the backpack I carry on campus

In this business-to-consumer example, the Visnostic Statements you choose for marketing tablet devices should focus on the most emotional wants and expectations of college students. Ideally, you would focus your statements to:

- Highlight aspirations such as never running out of battery power
- Identify emotional issues such as devices working like smartphones
- Surface chronic problems such as loosing access to the Internet

Think of three more Visnostic Statements relevant to this example and write them below.

VISNOSTIC STATEMENTS

HOW PLANSTARTGROW USES VISNOSTICS

PlanStartGrow (www.planstartgrow.com) is a marketing consultancy and agency for small and medium-sized businesses (SMBs) that I founded during 2012. While the following describes some of the challenges faced by consultancies, agencies, and businesses it also demonstrates the flexibility of VISNOSTICS and its ability to solve problems for marketers regardless of where they work.

A popular approach to B2B marketing success involves demonstrating how to save businesses money since this creates a tangible benefit. Yet, that's rarely what businesses want to speak about. Instead, they prefer to focus on long lists of projects and tasks they need help to complete.

Think about this for a moment and you will notice a flaw in the logic of this request—the probable reason a business considers help from an outside source (whether consultant, agency, contractor, freelancer, etc.) is they can't figure out how to better their marketing. Yet, in these cases many businesses self-diagnose their problems, self-prescribe solutions, and then select a third-party to implement these "fixes". This creates a scenario where a marketer gets paid to do exactly what the business orders and then later explains the inevitably disappointing results while assuring everyone it was the fault of no one involved.

This reminds me of the common practice of switch internet providers when another carrier promises a better experience, while knowing no meaningful change is likely to occur. Switching marketers is straightforward and this fosters a vicious cycle where marketers are periodically fired and replaced—with little progress made towards improving marketing.

VISNOSTICS offers a way to break this vicious cycle by helping businesses focus on their desirable outcomes, and this provides an opportunity for marketers to develop strategy to overcomes apparent and hidden marketing challenges.

Imagine that instead of asking a business what marketing help they needed, you asked them to envision a more successful business. During this process, they might consider the following open questions, for example:

- **Who** would be involved in making your business more successful?
- **What** would this mean to your owners and shareholders, employees and contractors, and suppliers and customers?
- **When** could this occur, and would it happen all-at-once or in stages?
- **Where** are the resources to support change, and are they accessible?
- **Why** would this be worthwhile effort for the business and positive experience for you?
- **How** would you build a roadmap and begin the journey along its path?

These types questions or prompts focus participants on strategic initiatives that create lasting business value rather than tactical activities offering near-term benefits. PlanStartGrow uses open questions like the ones above in conjunction with VISNOSTICS whenever possible.

ALMOST FREE MARKETING® AND VISNOSTICS

At PlanStartGrow, we use VISNOSTICS to introduce and describe our Almost Free Marketing system, the best way to maximize the effectiveness and optimize the efficiency of marketing.

Marketing involves influencing behavior in order for someone to get a chance at trading goods and services with someone else. Customary marketing practices often begin with costly research-based processes for determining the needs, wants, and expectations of markets. This is followed by slow communications-based processes that explain why your business is the best alternative for potential customers and clients. The emphasis is usually on needs in a business-to-business environment or wants in a business-to-consumer one, and everyone insists on having their expectation met. Therefore, anything that can help a marketer to influence behavior is valuable.

Here the Top 10 Visnostic Statements we currently use when discussing Almost Free Marketing, though I'm certain these questions will continue to evolve using the principles of VISNOSTICS:

Responses
- A – I can say this today!
- B – I wish I could say this today.
- C – It's not important, not applicable, or I don't know.

VISNOSTIC STATEMENTS: Almost Free Marketing
We can make money by boosting sales revenue while maintaining marketing budget.
We can save money by cutting marketing budget while maintaining sales revenue.
We know the actual marketing activities contributing to signing our largest customers.

VISNOSTIC STATEMENTS: Almost Free Marketing
We know the actual marketing activities contributing to closing our most profitable deals.
We know the actual marketing activities contributing to building our best sales pipeline.
We can predict which marketing qualified leads will become sales qualified leads.
We can predict which marketing contacts will become marketing qualified leads.
We understand the individual effectiveness and efficiency of marketing campaigns.
We have a roadmap to follow for maximizing marketing effectiveness.
We have a roadmap to follow for optimizing marketing efficiency.

An important thing to notice about these diagnostics statements is that they extend to include three topics of shared interest: 1) the *strategic business issues* of profit, revenue, and budgets, 2) the *tactical sales issues* of customers, deals, and pipeline, and 3) the *tactical marketing issues* of leads, contacts, campaigns, and roadmaps. Success is best achieved with a multi-disciplinary team including members of the management, marketing, and sales staff, so evaluating these diagnostics statements *intentionally requires* the participation of all three business disciplines.

Businesses mostly respond with "I wish I could say this today" to these Visnostic Statements for Almost Free Marketing. Whenever we hear a response of "it's not important, not applicable, or I don't know", we explore the topic behind that Visnostic Statement to understand why that response was chosen. Similarly, when we get a response of "I can say this today" we confirm the statement was understood as intended and then validate the reasons for the response.

Almost Free Marketing helps any business to gain the capability to respond to all of these and other Visnostic Statements with "I can say this today".

EXERCISE: Create Visnostic Statements for Almost Free Marketing

You may be surprised by how simple this exercise can be even if you are unfamiliar with Almost Free Marketing. All you really need to know before you get started is that Almost Free Marketing focuses on two things: 1) making marketing more effective, and 2) making marketing more efficient. Therefore, your Visnostic Statements are effectively 'wish list items' related to marketing effectiveness and efficiency. Thinking about one business you know will help.

- Sample Visnostic Statement for extreme effectiveness: *'My business can generate more leads than it can use.'*

- Sample Visnostic Statement for extreme efficiency *'My business can do all of its marketing with one person.'*

Now, write a few realistic Almost Free Marketing Visnostic Statements of your own and then ask someone at your company to provide a response (A, B, or C) for each one. For extra credit, individually ask different people for responses and compare the results.

Responses
- A – I can say this today!
- B – I wish I could say this today.
- C – It's not important, not applicable, or I don't know.

VISNOSTIC STATEMENTS

SUCCESS EIGHT
ON-GOING READER SUCCESSES

In addition to Omar's marketing business, several other readers are currently developing multiple joint efforts with Visnostics.

As I already shared in the Website Success Section, Michael Bosworth immediately incorporated Visnostics into his Story Telling training business. His wife's marriage counseling company, WeConcile, also has some of the best Visnostic Statements I've ever seen.

Brand new companies like NeuroViews are popping up after reading Visnostics, people are starting to advertise homes very differently, I am starting to see things changing rapidly with dozens of other sales and marketing efforts and it's exciting!

People are THINKING differently. Eyes are finally seeing the silliness of forcing clients to translate features and functions into why they care!

FINALLY!

One of the ways that I hope to get more involved is in the world of Education! I've been working with John Kratz, Professor at the University of Minnesota

Duluth and he recently asked me if I would be interested in serving on his Board of Advisors. I hope this the first of MANY!

In addition, I'm also getting involved with the sales program at The University of Texas in Dallas.

When I originally asked Sherry Hall to read the draft of my first book, I envisioned she would provide editing suggestions only. However, she made this comment to me which is now include in the "Early Reaction" section of almost all my books:

Sherry Hall, Award-Winning Author, and Educator
"While Kim's work most certainly has the potential to be life-changing for salespeople, it also holds implications beyond the world of business. As an educator, I have seen first-hand the power of visualization. I believe Kim's groundbreaking book can create positive change across multiple settings."

Sherry's experience in the world of education has been invaluable and enlightening. She is currently co-writing a book with me and is in the research stage of her writing. I asked her if she wanted to submit anything for this book and this is what she provided me:

As an educator for over two decades, too often I have seen someone attempt to apply business principles to education and I know it just doesn't work. Education is different.

So, I was shocked to find myself highlighting and notating pages in Kim's book, Visnostic Selling, that spoke to me as an *educator. Those pieces that are so applicable to education spurred conversation that led to our partnership in creating **Visnostics for Teaching and Learning**.*

Sometimes in education when we see a student is not mastering what we are teaching, the temptation is to try again by delivering our content slower and louder. It doesn't work! We have to be able to choose multiple approaches and styles to meet each learner where they are.

We know what our content and student objectives are, and how valuable it is to our students. It can be baffling to us as educators when we have students in front of us that don't seem to care at all about what we have to teach them, all the knowledge we have to impart, or our beautiful lesson plan that we toiled over all weekend. Why does this happen?

*This powerful experiences Kim shared in this book have huge implications for us as educators. Think about how engaging it would be to have student buy-in and ownership of **their own learning**! And not just for their time in your classroom- but for the value it can add to their lives.*

*Kim poses the question: why do we need classrooms if we can just read books and learn the content? Why indeed. As educators, you know already that it takes much more than just reading a book in isolation to take on new skills. **Visnostics for Teachers and Learners** provides you with examples specific to the classroom setting. There is no age limit on learning and the application for educators spans all levels of educations.*

Visnostics for Teaching and Learning *coming soon!*

In addition to *Visnostics for Teaching and Learning*, I've talked with several readers about co-writing additional Visnostics Special Editions and the topics discussed so far include:

- **VISNOSTIC LEADERSHIP**
- **VISNOSTIC STORY TELLING**
- **VISNOSTICS BY AUDIENCE (DISC)**
- **VISNOSTIC MARKETING**

As I build my training business, I am looking for established training organizations to conduct Visnostic Workshops because I can't do this without a lot of help! And the demand is high because more and more companies are looking for new and different ways to sell and market to their prospective clients.

I say this multiple times in every single book – Please reach out to me. I have a vested interest in every single reader's success but I don't know you exist unless you write a review or message me!

Together, we can change the world – one Visnostic Statement at a time!

Happy Visnostics!

APPENDIX
Sales Basics Review, Tips, and Answers

Neuroscience Definition:

neu·ro·sci·ence

'n(y)o͞orō͵sīəns/

noun: **neuroscience**; plural noun: **neurosciences**

Any or all of the sciences, such as neurochemistry and experimental psychology, which deal with the structure or function of the nervous system and brain.

Neuroscience References:

Using Neuroscience to skyrocket sales

https://neilpatel.com/blog/7-neuroscience-principles-you-should-use-to-increase-sales/

Your Brain Prefers Cartoons over Photos

https://www.newyorker.com/culture/culture-desk/this-is-your-brain-on-cartoons/amp

5 Scientific Reasons Why Video Is Better

https://go.yumyumvideos.com/blog/5-scientific-reasons-why-online-video-engages-your-audience

Why Questions and Surveys annoy clients

https://www.mycustomer.com/community/blogs/wizu/7-reasons-why-your-customers-hate-your-surveys

The Neuroscience of Selling – INC magazine

https://www.inc.com/geoffrey-james/the-neuroscience-of-selling.html

What Great Salespeople Do Summary

http://storyleaders.com/book/

More Science

https://blog.insidesales.com/inside-sales-thought-leaders/buyers-brain/

Basic Sales Psychology Principles:

Sales rejection is partially due to human natures resistance to being persuaded. Winning a point or argument is what humans want and need.

Body Language Basics:

Looking to Their Right = Auditory Thought
(Remembering a song)
Looking to Their Left = Visual Thought
(Remembering the color of a dress)
Looking Down to Their Right =
Someone is creating a feeling or sensory memory
(Thinking what it would be like to swim in Jell-O)
Looking Down to Their Left = Someone talking to themselves

Pain Drives Buyers - Good Pain and Bad Pain:

People buy due to pain (GOOD pain is caused by things like rapid growth, lack of resources, supply chain issues, etc. and BAD pain is caused by things like no growth, layoffs necessary, too much stock, etc.) A good salesperson will be attempting to uncover pain throughout the sales process.

Business Terminology:

B2B – Business to Business –
When a company sells to another company.
Example: A computer manufacturer will sell wholesale to a retail store versus the consumer.
B2C – Business to Consumer –
When a company sells to the end-user.
Example: When a retail store sells directly to the consumer.

Visnostic Book URL References:

"You Are Who You Are Because Where You Were When"

https://www.youtube.com/watch?v=_aY163kwlW4

"7 Presentation Ideas That Work for Any Topic."

https://www.inc.com/carmine-gallo/7-presentation-ideas-that-work-for-any-topic.html

"The Rule of Threes"

https://www.youtube.com/watch?v=SY23zi1u_3U

SlideShare

https://www.slideshare.net

DynaExec Visnostic Statements

https://www.surveymonkey.com/r/TR73SMS

Kimberlee Slavik

https://www.linkedin.com/in/kimslavik

DynaExec Website Video

https://player.vimeo.com/video/353714183

Michael Bosworth

https://www.linkedin.com/in/mikebosworth/

David A. Wiener

https://www.linkedin.com/in/david-a-wiener-573b1a1/

David's artwork

http://artbydavidwiener.blogspot.com

The Art of Answering Questions:

Never ask closed-ended questions – Yes and No answers can be blurted out without any thought behind the answer. Open-ended questions have problems as well because they can go in many different directions and you lose focus on the original intent. Having multiple-choice is the best way for the audience to ponder and consider the options. They have to think harder to answer, which is how you get people emotionally engaged.

Studies have shown that giving people options, triggers chemicals in the brain to choose one. For example – if you say "Will you buy from me?" Yes or No? It is way too easy to say No. However, if you give your client THREE pricing/package options from which to choose, they will typically choose one. So it is an automatic YES. So when I am responded to an RFP (Request for Proposal), RFI (Request for Information, or an RFQ (Request for Quotation), I always provide three alternative pricing scenarios. The theory is that they will choose one of the three options vs. eliminating you from the other bids.

Questions Continued - Very Important Point:

When a client asks a question, you will automatically want to answer it. Instead, ask what is driving that specific question. Often, the real question is not what the client actually asked. When I go on sales calls with a Software Engineer, Technical Support, Management, or other teammates, their purpose for being on the call is usually to answer all questions sales can't handle. However, when questions arise, it is imperative to uncover what is driving the question so you don't get drug down the wrong path and derail the momentum of the meeting.

For example, I was in a meeting about three weeks before Thanksgiving and the client asked what was the average implementation time. This is a logical question and my engineer wanted to tell the client that the answer was six weeks. Instead of answering the question, I asked the client why this question was important and they responded with they wanted to make sure it could be completed before the holidays (which I just said was in three weeks). If we had answered the question with the "six weeks" response, the client would have jumped to the conclusion that we were not the appropriate solution and we would have lost the sale.

The real question the client wanted to ask was, "Could you have this implemented by the holidays?" And our answer would have been, "Yes, we will double up on resources to ensure implementation is complete by the holidays."

Company and book sites:

www.dynaexec.com

www.visnostics.com

www.visnosticselling.com

Buy Books:

Memoirs of an Angry Sales Pro – Sales Leadership MUST Change!

https://www.amazon.com/Memoirs-Angry-Sales-Pro-Leadership/dp/1733194630/ref=sr_1_1?keywords=memoirs+of+an+angry+sales+pro&qid=1568169902&s=gateway&sr=8-1

Visnostics Special Edition for Real Estate

https://www.amazon.com/Visnostics-Neuroscientific-Approach-Communicating-Marketing/dp/1733194614/ref=sr_1_2?keywords=visnostic+selling&qid=1566930437&s=gateway&sr=8-2

Visnostics Special Edition for Auto Sales

https://www.amazon.com/Visnostics-VISualization-DiagNOSTIC-Neuroscientific-Communicating/dp/1733194649/ref=sr_1_3?keywords=visnostic+selling&qid=1566930437&s=gateway&sr=8-3

Visnostic Selling
(Replaced with Visnostic Sales and Marketing)
https://www.amazon.com/Visnostic-Selling-neuroscientific-marketing-leadership/dp/1732191611/ref=sr_1_1?keywords=visnostic+selling&qid=1566930399&s=gateway&sr=8-1

Podcasts and Other URLs:
Visnostic Podcasts, Education, and Speaking:

July 19, 2019 – Donald C. Kelly, The Sales Evangelist
The Fundamentals of Visnostic Selling
https://www.stitcher.com/podcast/donald-kelly/the-sales-evangelist-sales-trainingspeakingbusiness-marketingdonald/e/62674347

June 18, 2019 – Brian Burns, The Brutal Truth About Sales Basic Visnostics – Statements NOT Questions
https://www.stitcher.com/podcast/brian-burns/the-brutal-truth-about-sales-selling/e/61931321?autoplay=true

April 22, 2019 – Dr. Pelè, Big Ticket Clients
Basic Visnostics
https://www.youtube.com/watch?v=FbW-sSu4BOo&t=304s

Current CEO DynaExec Introduction to Visnostics
https://player.vimeo.com/video/353714183

Visnostics in Seven Seconds
https://www.youtube.com/watch?v=dy5s4kYWdjY.

Potential Answers to Exercise #4
1. I saved **$150,000** per year within **six** months of purchasing new software.
2. The ROI was **12x** what I paid for the software in under **eighteen months** of the purchase.
3. Revenues increased by **$12,000,000** in under **two** years due to increased client demand.
4. Client satisfaction is at an all-time high thanks to **automation**.
5. **We now have a competitive advantage in the marketplace** within **six months** but more importantly; our new service is giving our clients a **competitive advantage** as well.
6. I am able to say we had an implementation that caused **zero downtime**.
7. I was promoted due to **all these exciting improvements in our business**.
8. Highlight all results and timelines in 1-7.
9. Which numbers had no Results or Timelines?
   a. **They ALL had results but only 1,2,3,and 5 had timelines.**

NOTE: These are POTENTIAL answers. Your answers may be different and still be correct. The point of this exercise is to help you with the Visnostic THOUGHT PROCESS.

WORKSHOPS

In addition to Fractional Leadership that can be contracted for a day, week, month, quarter, or an entire year, there are three workshops that help DynaExec clients execute three major principles taught in the best-selling book, *Visnostic™ Sales & Marketing*.

First, vendor-centric marketing messaging must be translated and converted into client-centric Visnostic Statements. This is accomplished by working with sales and marketing during a ***Translation Workshop***. This is the fundamental workshop needed to create stronger messaging. This workshop eliminates the need for clients to translate features and functions and other jargon into "why they care." This is accomplished by doing the work for them. This workshop converts current messaging into dialogue that will improve your clients' comprehension and retention of your messaging. In addition, you will strengthen your rapport with your clients because they will FEEL positive emotions while engaging with your sales organization. Your sales organization will be able to quickly identify the clients' non-strength areas in which your company can convert to strengths.

Once the translation is completed and 10-20 strong "Visnostic Statements" are created per segmentation, the next step is the **Solution Mapping Workshop**. This second workshop is conducted with a more technical team while reviewing the Visnostic Statements created during the Translation Workshop.

Often, these second sets of eyes will identify and create additional Visnostic Statements to the ones Sales and Marketing identified during the Translation Workshop. In addition, this second group tend to enhance the newly created statements with powerful results they have observed during their post sales efforts. These final Visnostic Statements are then mapped to various Statement of Work descriptions that will describe HOW any "non-strengths" uncovered during the client discussion can become strengths. These Statement of Work descriptions are created during the Solution Mapping Workshop.

The final stage of the Visnostic transformation is to take the Visnostic Statements and the Statement of Works and complete a tool that will be given to the entire sales organization. Imagine a sales team that is in front of the client with a tablet, documenting the client responses. And residing on the tablet is a tool that will automatically produce an

"Insight Report" that will give your clients a recipe for success INSTANTLY!

This will eliminate the need for technical resources to be engaged early in the sales cycle. The client will see exactly how your company will turn their non-strengths into strengths!
The third workshop is *Visnostic Selling*, which is conducted with the entire sales organization to ensure they are each experts with the tool and they are well prepared to properly engage with the client.

Your sales organization will be CONFIDENT and COMPETENT in front of potential clients from their first WEEK in their sales role!

Here are the three workshops in greater detail -

_____

✦ *Client-Centric Translation For Sales & Marketing*

Objective –
Conversion is a form of translation. Converting features and functions into VISualization DiagNOSTIC (aka Visnostic) Statements is the act of translating vendor-centric wording (vendor-speak) into client-centric statements (client-speak) that clients can relate. DynaExec will assess current marketing tools & combine details from multiple sources to create Visnostic Statements & compatible visuals & graphics that enhance retention.

Attendees –
Sales and Marketing (Up to twelve participants)

Pre-requisites, Planning, and Preparation for Workshop –

- **Read *Visnostic Selling* Book** – (Preface, Chapters 1-3) Retail Price - $24.95 Workshop Discounted Rate - $19.95
- **Meeting #1** – Assessment - Conference Call to hear Presentation & Record for transcription (obtain script)
- **Meeting #2** – Assessment Results Revealed. Kick-off conference call after book is read but prior to workshop to set expectations
- **Meeting #3** – Onsite 8 hour Translation Workshop
  - ✓ CHAPTER ONE – Believing is Doing and Introduction (30 minutes)
  - ✓ Exercise #1 – "XXXX" exercise.
  - ✓ Slide presentation using graphics vs words
  - ✓ 3 graphics versus letters exercise – 3 seconds per slide Generation Z get timer added to PPT
  - ✓ CHAPTER TWO – Segmentation and why it is important. (30 minutes)
  - ✓ CHAPTER THREE – Solution Dissection. (1 hour)
  - ✓ CHAPTER FOUR – Translation (1 hour)
  - ✓ CHAPTER FIVE – Creating & Rating Visnostic Statements with Post It Notes by Segmentation. The importance of RTH. Use highlighters to identify, Reword if necessary. Prioritize. (1 hour working lunch)
  - ✓ CHAPTER SIX – Vertical and Target Market Strategies with Visnostic Statements (1 hour)
  - ✓ CHAPTER SEVEN – Class Presentations. Time will be determined based upon number of companies in each session and flexibility of class.
  - ✓ CHAPTER EIGHT – Conclusion and discussion of two additional workshops to create the tool. Demo of tool.
- **Ongoing Meetings (up to 30 days)** – Ensure success and document results are included in the workshop price.

Supplies Needed for In-Person Workshop –
- Conference Room with projection and white board
- Phone for call-in participants
- Internet
- Post-it Notes supplied by DynaExec
- Highlighters supplied by DynaExec

★ Mapping Segmentation Solution Workshop for Post Sales Roles

Objective –

After the feedback from the client is collected, a deliverable must be created that maps all "NON-STRENGTHS" identified with Visnostic Statements. It is important to not simply map products or services names to the areas in which can be strengthened. This workshop will summarize HOW your company will help clients improve their current situations. The result will be a client deliverable called an Insight Report.

Attendees –

Technical Team such as Software Engineers, Implementers, Support, Compliance, etc. (Up to twelve participants)

★ Visnostic Sales and Marketing Workshop

Objective –

After the first two workshops, a sales tool will be completed that converted features/functions and other technical jargon into statements the client can reflect and visualize. Sales will learn how to deliver this approach in lieu of a traditional sales presentation. Sales will learn how to use the new tool designed to create the Client Insight Report. Salespeople need to be entertained to learn. This workshop will have games and prizes as a shorter version of both previous workshops is conducted to ensure the sales organization understands basic Visnostics and the science behind why it works so well.

Attendees –
Sales and Sales Leadership (Up to twelve participants)
In less than 30 days and three workshops, with Visnostic Selling, your sales, marketing, and leadership will be transformed into Client Business Strategists. Furthermore, your clients will no longer avoid your teams' sales efforts because they will be viewed as a valuable extension of your client's own teams.

★ Additional Information

Workshops can be conducted in public forums or in private sessions.

The benefit of group forums is that during your presentation to the group, you will be educating other companies on the benefits, results, and differentiators of your company, which could result in new clients.

TIP – Companies that send representatives from both marketing and sales will benefit the most from the Translation Workshop, which is the most popular and fundamental way to strengthen the effectiveness of the messaging.

★ Assessment of Current Messaging – Pricing Options

ASSESSMENT - $1,500
This includes approximately 10 hours of consulting work prior to the in-person workshop. Cost of the Assessment will be applied to any future consulting services and workshops.

1. Read at the minimum, Preface and Chapters 1-3. (2 hours)
2. Record your best presentation (30 min max) on Zoom with slides.
3. Transcribe the presentation. (3 – 5 hours)
4. Bring four different highlighter pens (blue, yellow, pink, and green are preferred).
5. Be prepared to discuss your top five differentiators over your competition. (1 hour of research)
6. Download app – Poll Everywhere

POST WORKSHOP - $500/month retainer for consulting services.

Visnostic Sale and Marketing Readers and Pod Cast audience may contact podcast@DynaExec.com for *a free assessment ($1,500 value).* *

When was the last time you purchased a $25 book and received $1,500 of consulting for FREE?
*Special Pricing is for a Limited Time Only

BIOGRAPHIES
Author Bio and Resumé

Kimberlee Slavik –
https://www.linkedin.com/in/kimslavik

Kimberlee is an award-winning business strategist in the Information Technology (IT) industry, known for helping clients increase sales and profits by leveraging software, services, hardware, storage, business continuity, & cloud computing.

Currently CEO of DynaExec.
Member of several advisory boards.

Results:
- ✓ Sold or participated in selling over $1.9 billion worth of software, products, & services during a 30-year career
- ✓ Best Selling Author and inventor of Visnostic Selling Series
- ✓ Exceeded quota for 26 years of a 30 year career averaging almost 200% of plan
- ✓ Award Winning Global Sales Leader
- ✓ Over 85 unsolicited recommendations on LinkedIn from clients, peers, direct reports, indirect reports, and management validating accomplishments
- ✓ Exceeded $900 million dollar revenue objectives while managing a complex, 70+ person storage team with P&L (Profit and Loss) accountability for HP
- ✓ Recipient of numerous sales awards by focusing on post-sales support and customer references

Specialties:
- ✓ Surpassing sales objectives
- ✓ Inspirational Leadership Style
- ✓ Marketing and Sales Liaison
- ✓ Expert at selling intangible offerings
- ✓ Excellent post-sales client relationships
- ✓ Member of multiple advisory boards
- ✓ Training and education development and execution
- ✓ Transforming salespeople into top performers
- ✓ Exceptional business acumen & P&L (Profit and Loss)
- ✓ 15 years of people leadership
- ✓ Excellent communication & presentation skills
- ✓ Key Note Speaker
- ✓ Collaborative team player leading multiple teams towards a common goal
- ✓ Project management & organizational skills
- ✓ Organizational design & coaching high-performance teams
- ✓ Enterprise channel strategy development & execution
- ✓ C-level executives & senior execs sales closures
- ✓ Indirect enterprise channel sales & marketing
- ✓ Expertise in technology – including SaaS (Software as a Service), cloud, storage, virtualization, & business continuity

Education:
- ✓ Summa Cum Laude from LeTourneau University, with a Bachelor of Science degree in Business Administration.
- ✓ Certified by Southern Methodist University in "Leading the High-Performance Sales Organization."
- ✓ Currently pursuing an MBA degree in International Business at Heriot-Watt Business School in Edinburgh, Scotland.

Foreword Bio and Resumé

Michael Bosworth –
https://www.linkedin.com/in/mikebosworth/

Mike Bosworth has been a thought leader within the field of sales and marketing over the last several decades. He is an author, speaker, entrepreneur, story seeker and sales philosopher. Bosworth is the best-selling author of Solution Selling: Creating Buyers in Difficult Selling Markets (McGraw-Hill, 1993) co-author of Customer Centric Selling (McGraw-Hill, 2003) and co-author of What Great Salespeople Do: The Science of Selling Through Emotional Connection and The Power of Story (McGraw-Hill, 2012).

Mike Bosworth began his career in the information technology industry in 1972 on the Help Desk for Xerox Computer Services. He was their top new business salesperson in 1975, managed the "Branch of the Year" in 1979 and was promoted to Manager of Field Sales in 1980.

From 1976 through 1982 he designed and delivered sales training programs for Xerox's Computer Services Division. His years of field experience plus the knowledge he gained from working with Neil Rackham on the Xerox SPIN selling pilot project inspired him to found Solution Selling in 1983 with a mission to lift the bottom 80%. Solution Selling became one of the most widely adopted "customer usage training" methodologies in the technology industry.

In 2008, Mike realized that there was still a 'missing link' in understanding why such a small percentage of sellers generate such a large percentage of revenue. Mike's interest and research into how the very best sales professionals have high EQ and intuitively connect and build trust with buyers. This led him to build a framework around how to help the "bottom 80% boost their EQ with a connection framework based on the power of story." Mike founded Mike Bosworth Leadership in January 2013 to begin teaching salespeople and leaders to boost their EQ by using the power of storytelling and story tending to gain trust, and to influence without having to resort to using authority.

Bosworth has a degree in Business Management and Marketing from California State Polytechnic University.
In addition to his keynote speaking for professional associations and major corporations, he has been a featured lecturer at the Stanford Graduate School of Business, The Stanford Program on Market Strategy for Technology-Based Companies, The American Marketing Association Customer Message Management Forums, The Anderson School of Management At UCLA, the Paul Merage School of Business at UC Irvine, The University of Connecticut and Rollins College to name a few.

He lives with his wife Jennifer Lehr on Orcas Island, Washington.

Artist Bio and Resumé

David A. Wiener –
https://www.linkedin.com/in/david-a-wiener-573b1a1/

David is an action-oriented generalist with diverse sales and marketing experience in high technology environments. After engineering design and system installation of cryogenic systems, he entered the selling world of investment brokerage of large apartment buildings.

Then, after a decade of real estate investment, he moved to the high tech industry. He has a strong focus on business start-up, market expansion, and turnaround situations. He demonstrated success in sales and sales management of system and application software as well as hardware. He has been successful at small and large companies and divisions of large companies starting new ventures. He has held positions up to and including VP Sales. He has held a TS clearance and has expertise with systems integrators and government programs.

After his career in high tech, David moved on to small farm communities in Florida, Texas and then upstate New York where he built a studio and produces his art of fine ink drawings, oil paintings, and ceramics. He also spends his time working for his town as chair of the planning board. He also is a member of the County planning board and a board member of the town fire department.

Education: Newark College of Engineering - BSME, MSIE, MSCIS (abt)

For more information about David's artwork or to commission his talent, please visit http://artbydavidwiener.blogspot.com

CPSIA information can be obtained
at www.ICGtesting.com
Printed in the USA
LVHW021201071019
633402LV00001B/218/P

9 781733 194624